Lora & Company

**Fanciful
Characters
to Appliqué
by
Lora Rocke**

That
Patchwork
Place®

Credits

Editor-in-Chief .... Kerry I. Smith
Technical Editor .... Sally Schneider
Managing Editor .... Judy Petry
Copy Editor .... Liz McGehee
Illustrators .... Laurel Strand
Bruce Stout
Illustration Assistants .... Robin Strobel
Mary Ellen Buteau
Photographer .... Brent Kane
Design Director .... Cheryl Stevenson
Cover Designer .... Sandy Wing
Text Designer .... Amy Shayne
Design Assistant .... Marijane E. Figg

Lora & Company: Fanciful
Characters to Appliqué
© 1997 by Lora A. Rocke
That Patchwork Place, Inc., PO Box 118
Bothell, WA 98041-0118 USA

Printed in Hong Kong
02 01 00 99 98 97   6 5 4 3 2 1

Library of Congress Cataloging-in-Publication Data
Rocke, Lora.
    Lora & company : fanciful characters to appliqué /
        Lora A. Rocke. p. cm.
    ISBN 1-56477-150-4
    1. Machine appliqué — Patterns. 2. Patchwork —
Patterns. 3. Machine quilting. I. Title.
TT779.R63 1997   97-3653
746.46'041 — dc21   CIP

Dedication

To my loving husband, Roger, and daughter, Sean.

Acknowledgments

I couldn't have completed any of the designs without the love and nimble fingers of my mom, Barbara, who sewed the binding on every project. A special thank-you to Stephanie and Célest for their patience and loving support; to Rosie for her friendship and enthusiasm; to Janet and Kathi for their honesty; and to Kate, Gloria, and Teri for their encouraging words.

Table of Contents

Introduction

Quilting is a land of enchantment. The colors, the choices, and the designs all provide a wonderful place to escape to and to dream about. I have been an inhabitant of this land for almost twenty years. I have thrilled to the discovery of new patterns, new colors, and new possibilities for quilt creations. But, long before I ventured into quilting, I was fascinated with figures. When I found that I could translate what I drew into appliqué, my quilting world and my art world combined into an exciting adventure of form and function. As I have always loved the stories and the artwork of early-twentieth-century children's literature, it was only natural that I quilt the characters I have enjoyed. I created a world for them to inhabit, a place to live—a world of quilt blocks, fabric, and quilting designs.

Do you remember those wonderful imaginary figures from childhood? Besides the bogeyman and the tooth fairy, there was Jack Frost at your windowpane, leaving tell-tale signs of his passing. Have you ever felt the presence of a guardian angel, with silver wings made of stars? Or known that there must be others, more earthly, protecting small creatures, flowers, and ferns. Were there fairies in your garden using lightning bugs for street lamps? A heavenly jester fishing for wishes? Scarecrows dancing just like Fred Astaire? Santas on rooftops with presents for everyone? I know these people. Most of them were friends of mine while I was growing up.

Say hello to some old friends and meet some of my new chums. Let them occupy a special place on your wall, decorating your home to make it feel friendly and warm, safe and protected. It's just like magic.

One of my favorite mottoes is "It doesn't have to look simple to be simple." My designs are made using basic quiltmaking techniques with as little fuss as possible. I use the timesaving methods of rotary cutting, strip piecing, machine appliqué, and machine quilting throughout the book. I love the unexpected and the whimsical. If you look closely, you will find that I have used traditional blocks and fabrics in nontraditional ways, choosing a fabric to fit the design rather than the design to fit the fabric. I also like to hide little surprises within the design, usually in the quilting. It may be a bug, a spider, a snowflake, or reindeer hoof prints. You, too, can add to the mystery, magic, and joy of your quilt with some of your own personal touches.

As I teach classes and talk to quilters, I try to emphasize that everyone is creative. Creativity lies inside all of us, waiting for the opportunity to show itself. Use the patterns in this book to spark your creative engine. Experiment with a new color combination or sewing technique. These designs will provide a challenge at some level for quilters of all abilities. Take your time, and you, too, can complete any of these quilts—just like magic.

Tools and Supplies

Keep these basic sewing tools handy: pins, a seam ripper, scissors, and good light. Additional supplies and equipment include:

Sewing machine: To machine piece, make sure your machine has a good straight stitch. If your machine has decorative stitches, especially the buttonhole stitch, you can use those too for appliqué and embellishing.

¼"-wide presser foot: Some machines have a special foot that measures exactly ¼" from the needle to each outer edge so you can use the edge of the foot as a guide while piecing. Use this if it is available for your machine. Otherwise, to determine accurate seam allowances, see page 9.

Walking foot: The walking foot, or even-feed foot, is designed to move the top fabric along at the same speed as the bottom fabric. Use it for machine quilting straight lines, diagonals, or gentle curves. Do not use it to quilt any lines that require turning around the entire quilt.

Darning foot: Use the darning foot for free-motion quilting techniques. You must drop the feed dogs on most machines to use the darning foot. I use this foot for virtually all of my quilting. It is especially useful for doodling and for quilting feathers, sharp angles, and turns. You can quilt in any direction without turning the entire quilt.

Rotary-cutting tools: You will need a rotary cutter with a sharp blade, a cutting mat, and acrylic rulers. I use a 6" Bias Square® ruler, and 3½" x 12" and 6½" x 24" rulers.

Needles: Always start a new project with a new needle. The needle you have been using may have invisible burrs or a blunt end. For machine piecing, choose size 80/12. Use size 70/10 or 80/12 for machine quilting. You can use size 60/8 with nylon thread.

Thread: For machine piecing, I recommend good 100% cotton thread (size 50/3) or cotton-wrapped polyester. For machine quilting, use 100% cotton machine-quilting thread (Mettler Silk Finish 100% cotton machine quilting thread is a good choice for both machine and hand quilting), machine-embroidery thread, or some of the decorative threads now available. Use regular-weight or machine-quilting thread in the bobbin. Invisible or smoke-colored nylon thread is also available at your local quilt shop; use this in the top of the machine only, not in the bobbin.

Different combinations of thread in the top and bobbin produce different effects. Test them before you begin to quilt your project. Practice on the same fabric and batting you are using for your project.

Template plastic: If you must cut more than one piece from a pattern, you may wish to make a template. Templates made from clear or frosted plastic are more accurate and durable than cardboard templates. The see-through quality of plastic makes tracing easy and precise.

Marking tools: Several types of marking tools are available today. Test your marking tool to make sure you can remove the marks from the fabric. For marking around templates and for quilting lines, use a sharp No. 3 pencil or a mechanical pencil. Use a gray or white pencil for darker colors. Chalk markers also work well, but the chalk tends to wear off with handling.

Appliqué Techniques

Note: All the appliqué techniques described produce a mirror-image design of the printed pattern. When tracing appliqué shapes, draw along the outside lines of the shape; then cut and sew along the outside of the drawn lines. This allows for the slight loss of fabric that occurs when you turn under the seam allowance.

Traditional Hand Appliqué

1. Trace the desired appliqué shape onto the wrong side of the chosen fabric. Cut out the appliqué shape ⅛" to ¼" from the drawn line.

2. Turn the seam allowance to the wrong side of the fabric. A narrower seam allowance (⅛") on tiny pieces makes handling easier. Baste around the piece along the fold. To keep inside curves smooth and points accurate, clip the seam allowance almost to the tracing line.

    Do not turn under edges that will be covered by other appliqué pieces. They should lie flat under the appliqué piece(s) that will be on top.

3. Pin or baste the appliqué pieces in the position indicated by the appliqué plan. Match the thread to the appliqué piece and use a tiny blind hemstitch to sew the pieces in place.

4. Start the first stitch from the wrong side, inserting the needle perpendicular to the fold. Catch one or two threads of the appliqué piece. Push the needle to the wrong side and travel parallel to the edge of the appliqué. Come up about ⅛" from previous stitching, catching one or two threads along the folded edge of the appliqué. Continue in the same manner around the entire appliqué piece.

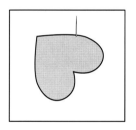 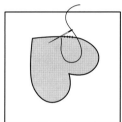

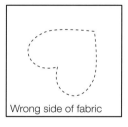

Wrong side of fabric

5. To remove excess fabric from behind the appliqué piece, carefully make a small slit in the center of the background fabric only, then trim the background ¼" from the stitching. Remove and discard the piece of background fabric.

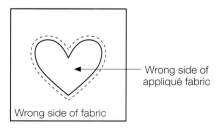

Wrong side of appliqué fabric

Wrong side of fabric

Machine Appliqué

Many sewing machines today feature an adjustable blind hemstitch or buttonhole stitch. Use thread that matches your appliqué piece or invisible nylon thread to appliqué the pieces in position. Pin or baste the appliqué pieces in place as indicated by the appliqué plan. Arrange the pieces so the appliqué is to the left of the needle. Adjust the width of the appliqué stitch so it is fairly small, and sew around the shape. To turn at a point or at an inside angle, stop with your needle in the down position, lift the presser foot, and turn the fabric. Continue sewing around the entire piece. Make sure any raw edges are covered.

Interfaced Appliqué

Use lightweight fusible interfacing to help turn under the edges of the appliqué shape and to hold it in place until it is appliquéd. You may use hand- or machine-appliqué methods.

1. Trace the design onto the wrong side of the appliqué fabric. Layer the fabric with the fusible interfacing, right sides together. (The right side of the interfacing is the dotted side.) Do not iron.

2. Pin to hold the pieces in place and sew on the traced line. Cut out the shape ⅛" to ¼" from the stitching. Do not sew edges that will be covered by other appliqué pieces; these edges are shown as dashed lines on the pattern pieces. Clip curves and inside angles; trim points.

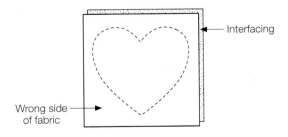

Interfacing

Wrong side of fabric

3. Turn the piece right side out through an open edge, or make a small slit in the center of the interfacing for turning. Smooth all edges and curves and carefully push out all points.

4. Arrange the pieces in the position indicated by the appliqué plan and fuse them in place using a hot steam iron. Machine or hand appliqué the shapes in place. To remove excess fabric from behind the appliqué piece, make a small slit in the center of the background fabric only. Trim the background ¼" from the stitching. Remove and discard the piece of background fabric and interfacing.

Fusible Appliqué

This is a quick and easy method because it is not necessary to sew the pieces to the background. Apply interfacing to any light-colored appliqué pieces to prevent a darker background from showing through the appliqué.

Choose a medium- to lightweight paper-backed fusible web, such as Wonder-Under® or HeatnBond®. Always follow the manufacturer's directions for iron temperature and pressing time.

1. Trace all appliqué pieces onto the paper side of the fusible web. Cut out the traced pieces, leaving about ⅛" of paper around each piece.

2. With the fusible web against the wrong side of the appliqué, fuse the shapes in place. Cut out the shapes on the tracing lines, then remove the paper backing, leaving a thin film of fusible web on the fabric.

3. Arrange the appliqué pieces in place as indicated by the appliqué plan, overlapping pieces where indicated. To help stabilize the appliqué pieces before final placement, place the appliqué pieces and background on a padded surface and push pins straight into the padding.

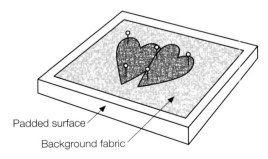

Padded surface

Background fabric

Fuse the appliqué pieces into position, removing the pins as you fuse.

Cutting & Piecing Techniques

Rotary Cutting

Use a rotary cutter, mat, and ruler to cut pieces for your quilts whenever possible, then sew them together by machine.

1. Fold the prewashed and pressed fabric along the lengthwise grain, matching the selvages. Place the folded edge closest to you on a cutting mat.

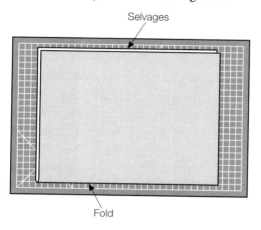

Selvages

Fold

2. With a long straight ruler on the left, and a Bias Square ruler on the right, align the Bias Square along the folded edge. Slide both rulers to the left almost to the raw edges. Remove the Bias Square and cut along the right edge of the long ruler, discarding the trimmed edges. (Reverse the process if you are left-handed.) Now you are ready to cut the required pieces from your fabric.

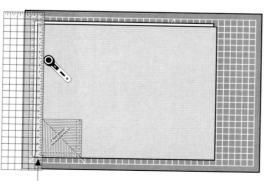

Trimmed edge

3. To cut strips, align the required measurement on the ruler along the cut edge of the fabric. Align one of the horizontal marks on the ruler along the fold of the fabric. This will ensure a straight strip. Rotary cut along the edge of the ruler.

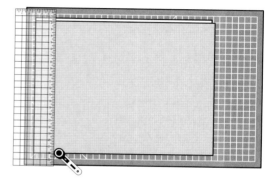

4. To cut squares, first cut strips the desired width. Trim away the selvage edges of the strip, align the required measurement on the ruler with the left edge of the strip, and cut a square. Continue cutting squares until you have the number needed for your project.

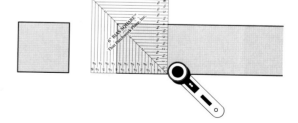

5. To cut half-square triangles, cut a square in half along the diagonal to make two triangles.

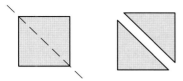

6. To cut quarter-square triangles, cut a square twice diagonally to make four triangles.

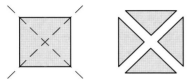

Machine Piecing

Accurate machine piecing depends on stitching consistent ¼"-wide seam allowances. If your seam allowance is off even the tiniest bit, your finished blocks will not be the correct size. Test the accuracy of your seams by measuring from the center of your stitching to the outside edge.

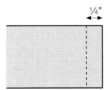

To determine where the ¼" measurement is on your machine, place a piece of ¼" graph paper under the machine needle. Push the needle through the graph paper just a tiny bit to the right of the first ¼" line. Place a piece of masking tape on the bed of your machine, next to the edge of the graph paper, for a seam guide. Make sure the tape does not cover the feed dogs.

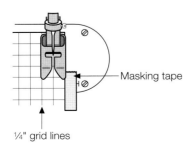

Masking tape

¼" grid lines

Chain Piecing

This is an efficient way to create several units a section at a time. Set your stitch length at 12 to 15 stitches per inch. Place two fabric pieces, right sides together, under the presser foot. Sew them together, using a ¼"-wide seam allowance. Without cutting the thread or lifting the presser foot, slide in the next pair and stitch the seam. There is no need to backstitch. Continue in this manner until you have stitched each pair together. Remove the chain from the machine. Press all seams on the wrong side to set the stitches. Clip the threads between the pieces, then press the seams in the desired direction from the right side.

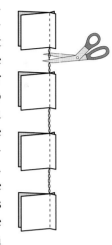

Opposing Seams

The traditional rule for pressing seams is to press them toward the darker fabric whenever possible. If you plan your pressing so the intersecting seams lie in opposite directions, the two seams will naturally butt up against each other, making it easier to match seams. In each quilt plan, I have indicated the pressing direction of the joining seams to increase accuracy and to reduce bulk at seam intersections.

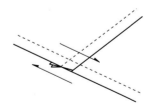

Press opposing seams in opposite directions before joining.

Quick Corners

Some of the blocks featured in this book are made of rectangles or squares with triangular corners of a contrasting fabric.

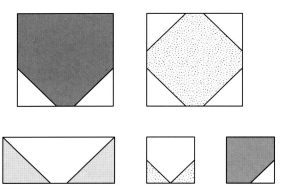

Use squares instead of triangles to piece these units, following the directions below. Quick-pieced corners require a little more fabric, but the savings in time and energy make it worthwhile.

To quick-piece the corners of a square, follow the cutting directions for your project to cut the required base square and the contrasting squares.

1. On the wrong side of the contrasting squares, draw a diagonal line from corner to corner.
2. Place a contrasting square on the corner of the base square, right sides together. Stitch along the diagonal line from outside edge to outside edge.
3. Trim the excess fabric from the contrasting square only, leaving a ¼"-wide seam allowance.
4. Press the resulting triangle toward the corner of the square. Repeat for the remaining corners as required for your project.

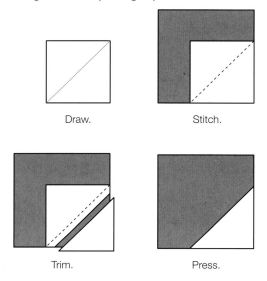

Draw.   Stitch.

Trim.   Press.

Quick Flying Geese

Cut the base rectangles and contrasting squares as indicated in the directions for your project.

1. On the wrong side of the contrasting squares, draw a diagonal line from corner to corner. Place a contrasting square on the corner of the base rectangle, right sides together.
2. Stitch along the diagonal line from outside edge to outside edge.
3. Trim the excess fabric from the contrasting square only, leaving a ¼"-wide seam allowance.
4. Press the resulting triangle toward the corner of the rectangle. Repeat the process on the other end of the rectangle to make one flying-geese unit.

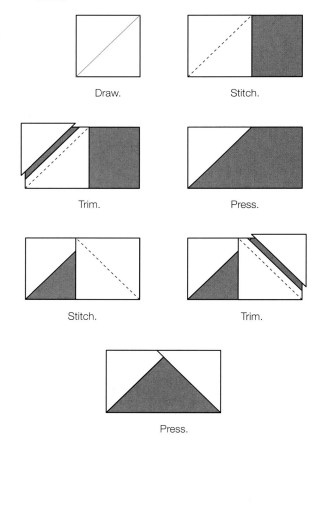

Draw.   Stitch.

Trim.   Press.

Stitch.   Trim.

Press.

Half-Square Triangle Units

Quick-Pieced Method

To make a small number of half-square triangle units or ones that are 2" square or smaller, I prefer to use this quick-piecing method. Trimming only one layer stabilizes the half-square triangle unit. Follow the cutting requirements for your project to cut identically sized squares of contrasting fabrics.

1. Draw a diagonal line on the wrong side of the lighter fabric. Place the fabrics right sides together and sew on the diagonal line.
2. Trim the excess fabric from only one of the contrasting squares, leaving a ¼"-wide seam allowance.
3. Press the resulting triangle toward the corner of the backing square to make one half-square triangle unit.

Stitch.   Trim.   Press.

Grid Method

To make a larger number of half-square triangle units, the grid method is fast. The resulting half-square triangle units are slightly larger than the required size, allowing a little extra to trim them to the correct size. Each square on the grid yields two half-square triangle units.

1. Cut two identically sized pieces of fabric and place them right sides together.
2. Determine the size of the squares for the grid by adding 1" to the finished size of your half-square triangle unit.

3. On the wrong side of the lighter fabric, draw a horizontal line the calculated distance from the edge.

4. Line up your ruler with the short edge of the fabric and measure the required distance for a square. Draw a vertical line. Repeat to the end of the fabric.

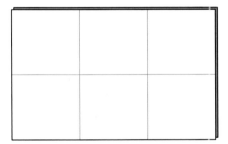

5. Draw diagonal lines through the squares in every other row in one direction; alternate the direction of the lines in the remaining rows so you can sew along the lines without having to cut your thread. Pin the two fabrics together to keep them from slipping while you stitch.

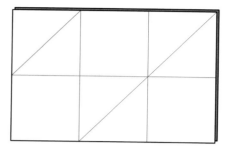

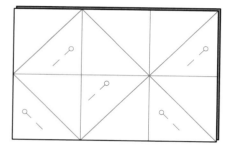

6. Begin sewing in one corner. Place the right edge of your presser foot on the diagonal line and sew to where it intersects the end of a straight line. Stop your needle in the down position. Lift the presser foot and rotate the fabric 90°, then continue sewing to the next corner. Rotate and repeat until you reach the opposite corner.

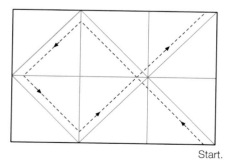

Start.

7. Repeat step 6 on the opposite side of the diagonal lines. When you finish, you should have a sewn line on either side of each diagonal line.

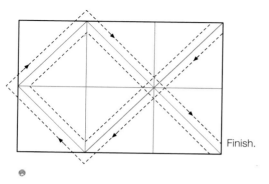

Finish.

8. Press the grid flat, then cut it apart on each drawn line, cutting the horizontal and vertical lines first, then the diagonal lines. Open each triangle and carefully press the seam to one side to avoid distorting the square.

9. Use the Bias Square to square up and trim each half-square triangle unit to the size required in your project.

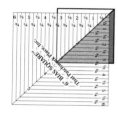

Trim half-square triangle units to the proper size.

Gallery of Quilts

Jack Frost
by Lora A. Rocke, 1995, Lincoln, Nebraska, 28" x 38".

Jest Wish
by Lora A. Rocke, 1996, Lincoln, Nebraska, 28" x 28".

Fairy Garden
by Lora A. Rocke, 1995, Lincoln, Nebraska, 35" x 49".

Star-Spangled Salute
by Lora A. Rocke, 1995, Lincoln, Nebraska, 32" x 42".

Fred A. Scarecrow

by Lora A. Rocke, 1995, Lincoln, Nebraska, 33" x 51".

Hello Santa!

by Lora A. Rocke, 1995, Lincoln, Nebraska, 22" x 32".

Guardian Angel

by Lora A. Rocke, 1996, Lincoln, Nebraska, 37" x 37".

Earth Angel

by Lora A. Rocke, 1996, Lincoln, Nebraska, 17" x 24".

Jack Frost

Materials: *44"-wide fabric*

⅝ yd. white print for hands, face, windows, and inner and outer borders

1 yd. gray print #1 for figure and inner border

½ yd. gray print #2 for background

⅝ yd. black print #1 for windows and inner border

⅞ yd. black print #2 for window sashings, inner border, and binding

¼ yd. black print #3 for scarf, shoe, hat, and pouch

⅜ yd. gray-and-black print for inner and outer borders

¼ yd. fusible interfacing

32" x 42" piece of batting

1 yd. for backing

Cutting

Use the patterns on pages 61–62 and on the pullout. Cut and prepare all appliqué shapes (figure, shoe, hat, hands, face, pouch, and scarf), using your favorite appliqué method (pages 6–7). Rotary cut the remaining pieces listed below.

From the white print, cut:
   5 squares, each 5" x 5", for windows
   2 squares, each 6" x 6", for inner border half-square triangles
   1 rectangle, 3" x 6", for inner border half-square triangles
   3 strips, each 3" x 42"; crosscut 48 rectangles, each 1¾" x 3", for outer border

From gray print #1, cut:
   4 squares, each 6¼" x 6¼"; cut each square twice diagonally for 16 inner border triangles
   4 squares, each 3⅜" x 3⅜"; cut each square once diagonally for 8 inner border triangles
   4 squares, each 3" x 3", for inner border

From gray print #2, cut:
   1 rectangle, 14½" x 20½", for background
   1 rectangle, 11½" x 16½", for background

From black print #1, cut:
   5 circles, each 4" in diameter (template on the pullout page), for windows
   2 squares, each 6" x 6", for inner border half-square triangles
   1 rectangle, 3" x 6", for inner border half-square triangles
   3 strips, each 1¾" x 42"; crosscut 48 squares, each 1¾" x 1¾", for outer border

From black print #2, cut:
   2 strips, each 1½" x 42"; crosscut 9 pieces, each 1½" x 4½", and 4 pieces, each 1½" x 9½", for window sashings
   1 strip, 1½" x 42", for inner border
   1 piece, 20" x 20", for binding

From the gray-and-black print, cut:
   3 strips, each 1¼" x 42"; crosscut 20 pieces, each 1¼" x 2¼", for inner border
   3 strips, each 1¾" x 42"; crosscut 52 squares, each 1¾" x 1¾", for outer border

Background

1. Using the 5" squares and 4" circles, make 20 Quick Drunkard's Path blocks as shown in the box at right. You will have 2 extra units.
2. Sew the Drunkard's Path blocks together in units of 2 or 4 as shown to create the window units.

Make 3.   Make 3.

3. Use 9 black pieces, each 1½" x 4½", and 4 black pieces, each 1½" x 9½", for the window sashings. Sew the window units together as shown to create a 9½" x 16½" section.

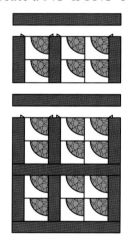

4. Join the window section to the long edge of the 11½" x 16½" background fabric. Press the seam toward the background. Add the remaining background piece to the top edge; press the seam toward the background.

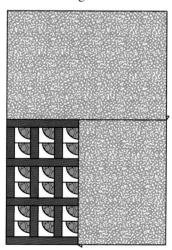

Quick Drunkard's Path Blocks

Create a Drunkard's Path block without piecing a curved seam, using fusible interfacing and appliqué.

1. Place the circle fabric right sides together with the fusible side of the interfacing. Trace a circle of the required size on the wrong side of the circle fabric.

2. Stitch completely around the circle on the drawn line and cut ¼" outside the stitching line. Cut notches at ½" intervals through the seam allowance almost to the stitching line.

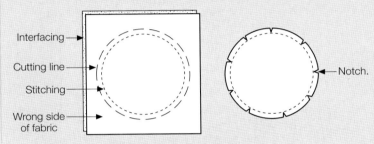

Interfacing
Cutting line
Stitching
Wrong side of fabric
Notch.

3. With scissors, cut a small X in the middle of the interfacing only. Turn the circle right side out through the X. Smooth the seams and finger-press along the turned edge. Place the circle, interfacing side down, in the center of the fabric square. Press with a steam iron to fuse the circle in place.

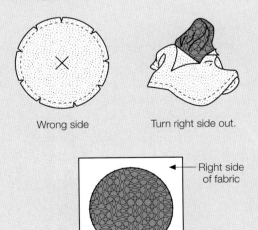

Wrong side

Turn right side out.

Right side of fabric

Appliqué.

4. Hand or machine appliqué, satin-stitch, or topstitch around the outer edge of the circle. Make a small slit behind the circle in the center of the background fabric only. Trim the background fabric and interfacing ¼" from the stitching.

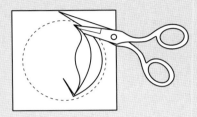

5. Cut the square into quarters as shown to make the Drunkard's Path unit, or leave it whole if the pattern requires an appliquéd circle.

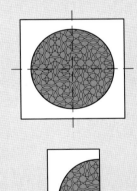

Pieced Borders

1. Sew a 1¼" x 42" gray-and-black strip to a 1½" x 42" black strip. Press the seam toward the black strip. Cut a total of 20 segments, each 1½" wide, from the strip unit.

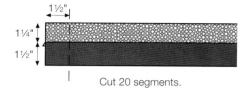

Cut 20 segments.

2. Add a 1¼" x 2¼" gray-and-black rectangle to each segment to make squares measuring 2¼" x 2¼".

Make 20.

3. Place each white 6" square right sides together with a black print 6" square. Repeat with the 3" x 6" rectangles. Mark a 3" grid on the wrong side of the white fabric. Following the directions for making half-square triangle units (pages 11–12), make 20 units. Trim them to 2½" x 2½".

Make 20.

4. Cut each half-square triangle unit in half diagonally, perpendicular to the seam line, to create 40 side-by-side triangles.

5. Sew a side-by-side triangle to 2 adjacent sides of each pieced square as shown to create 20 triangle units.

Make 20.

6. Arrange the triangle units with the gray quarter-square and half-square triangles as shown to create the top and bottom borders.

Top and Bottom Borders
Make 2.

7. Arrange the remaining triangle units with the gray quarter-square and half-square triangles and the gray 3" squares as shown to create the side borders.

Side Borders
Make 2.

8. Sew the top and bottom borders to the top and bottom edges of the quilt top; press these seam allowances and all remaining seam allowances toward the center. Sew the remaining borders to opposite side edges of the quilt top.

9. Using the 1¾" x 3" white rectangles, the 1¾" gray-and-black squares, and the 1¾" black print squares, quick-piece 48 flying-geese units (page 10). Add the two different black print squares at random.

Make 48.

10. Arrange the flying-geese units as shown to make the outer borders.

Top and Bottom Borders
Make 2.

Side Borders
Make 2.

Jack Frost

11. Sew the top and bottom borders to the quilt top; press the seams toward the quilt top. Sew the remaining borders to opposite sides of the quilt top, matching seams where necessary. Press the seams toward the quilt top.

Appliqué

1. Before appliquéing the face to the background, trace the facial features onto the right side of the fabric, using a permanent fabric marker.

2. Referring to the appliqué plan, position and appliqué each piece in numerical order.

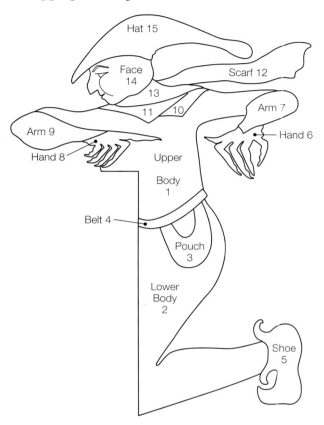

Finishing

Refer to "Finishing Techniques" on pages 57–60.

1. Layer the quilt top with batting and backing; baste.

2. Quilt as desired, or try one or more of the following ideas:
   * Outline-stitch around Jack Frost.
   * Doodle in the background.
   * Quilt snowflake designs in the background (pattern on pullout page).
   * Use metallic thread.
   * Quilt icicles hanging from Jack's hat, hands, elbows, and shoes. Quilt icicles in the borders or on the window sashings.

3. Add a hanging sleeve, bind the edges with double-fold bias binding, and add a label.

Guardian Angel

Materials: *44"-wide fabric*

⅞ yd. light blue print for background

⅜ yd. dark blue solid for World Star, border star, and inner border

⅜ yd. green print #1 for World Star

⅛ yd. green print #2 for gown and World Star

⅛ yd. medium blue solid for World Star

⅓ yd. gold print #1 for gown

1⅜ yds. gold print #2 for outer border, gown, and binding

⅛ yd. rose for face and hands

¼ yd. total assorted white prints for wings

9" x 9" square of gold lamé for halo

5" x 15" piece of burgundy print for gown

¼ yd. total assorted burgundy prints for hair

1¼ yds. for backing

41" x 41" piece of batting

Cutting

Use the patterns on the pullout page. Cut and prepare all appliqué shapes (face, hands, gown, hair, wings, and halo) from the appropriate fabrics, using your favorite appliqué method (pages 6–7). Rotary cut the remaining pieces listed below.

From the light blue print, cut:
   1 rectangle, 13½" x 14½", for background
   1 rectangle, 13½" x 27½", for background
   1 rectangle, 5" x 14", for World Star
   4 squares, each 2½" x 2½", for World Star

From the dark blue solid, cut:
   1 strip 3" x 42"; crosscut 1 rectangle, 3" x 6", for half-square triangle units, and 2 rectangles, each 3" x 10", for World Star and border star
   1 square, 2½" x 2½", for center of border star
   2 strips, each 1½" x 27½", for top and bottom borders
   2 strips, each 1½" x 29½", for side borders

From green print # 1, cut:
   1 strip, 2½" x 42"; crosscut 16 squares, each 2½" x 2½", for World Star
   1 rectangle, 5" x 14", for World Star

From green print #2, cut:
   2 rectangles, each 3" x 10", for World Star

From the medium blue solid, cut:
   1 rectangle, 3" x 10", for World Star
   1 square, 2½" x 2½", for center of World Star
   1 piece, 3" x 6", for half-square triangle units

From gold print #2, cut:
   1 rectangle, 3" x 10", for border star
   3 squares, each 2½" x 2½, for border star
   1 strip, 4½" x 27½", for left outer border
   1 strip, 4½" x 29½", for right outer border
   1 strip, 4½" x 31½", for top outer border
   1 strip, 4½" x 37½", for bottom outer border
   1 piece, 21" x 21", for binding

Background

1. Layer 1 dark blue and 1 green print #2 rectangle, each 3" x 10", right sides up. Fold them in half, aligning the edges. Trim the left side so the edges are even, then cut twice at 1⅞" intervals to make 4 rectangles, each 1⅞" x 3", of each color.

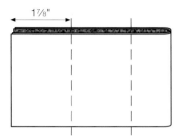

1⅞"

2. Cut each stack of rectangles diagonally to create 4 pairs of triangles. Sew pairs of triangles together as shown to form bias rectangles. Trim each bias rectangle to measure 1½" x 2½".

Make 4.   Make 4.

3. Repeat steps 1 and 2 with the medium blue solid and green print #2, and with the dark blue solid and gold print #2, for the border.

Make 4.   Make 4.

Make 4.   Make 4.

4. Sew pairs of dark blue and green bias-rectangle units together as shown. Repeat with the medium blue and green rectangles and the dark blue and gold #2 rectangles. Make 4 star points from each color combination. Reserve the dark blue/gold #2 units for the border star.

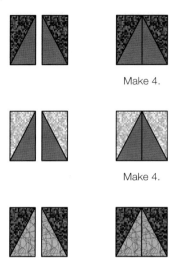

Make 4.

Make 4.

Make 4.

5. Layer the 5" x 14" rectangles of light blue print and green print #1 as you did in step 1 above. Fold the layers in half, trim the left edge, and cut twice at 2⅞" intervals to make 4 rectangles, each 2⅞" x 5", of each color.

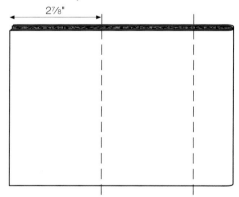

2⅞"

6. Cut each stack of rectangles diagonally to create 4 pairs of triangles. Sew pairs of triangles together as shown to form bias rectangles. Trim each rectangle to 2½" x 4½".

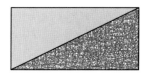

Make 4.

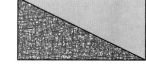

Make 4.

7. Place the 3" x 6" rectangles of dark blue and medium blue solids right sides together. Draw a 3" grid on the wrong side of the medium blue fabric. Make 4 half-square triangle units (pages 11–12). Trim them to 2½" x 2½".

Make 4.

8. Arrange the squares, half-square triangle units, and star points in rows as shown. Sew the rows together; press the seams in opposite directions from row to row. Sew the rows together. Trim the block, if necessary, to 14½" x 14½".

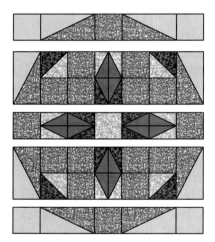

9. Sew the World Star block to the 13½" x 14½" piece of background fabric along the long edge. Press the seams toward the background fabric. Add the 13½" x 27½" background piece to the top edge; press the seams toward the background.

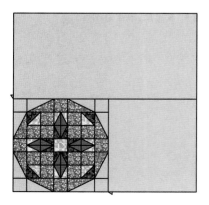

Appliqué

1. Before appliquéing the face to the background, trace the facial features onto the right side of the fabric, using a permanent fabric marker.

2. Referring to the appliqué plan below, position and appliqué each piece to the background in numerical order. Trim the appliqué edges even with the background.

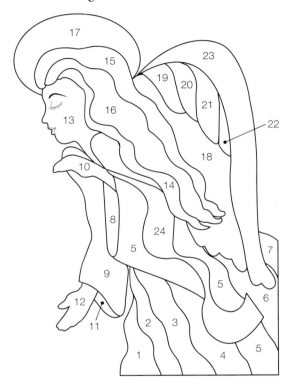

Borders

1. Pin the 1½" x 27½" strips of dark blue solid to the top and bottom edges of the quilt top. Match the center of the quilt top to the center of the border. Sew the borders and press all seams toward the dark blue border. Sew the 1½" x 29½" borders to opposite sides of the quilt top in the same manner.

2. Arrange the reserved star points with the plain border squares as shown. Sew them together to make the corner unit and the top of the left side border unit.

Make 1.

Make 1.

3. Join the left side border unit to the 4½" x 27½" gold print #2 strip as shown. Sew the border to the left side of the quilt top. Press the seam toward the border. Add the 4½" x 29½" gold print #2 strip to the right side.

4. Join the corner unit to the 4½" x 31½" gold print #2 strip. Press the seam toward the border. Sew the border to the top edge of the quilt top, matching the seams. Sew the 4½" x 37½" gold print #2 strip to the bottom.

Finishing

Refer to "Finishing Techniques" on pages 57–60.

1. Layer the quilt top with batting and backing; baste.

2. Quilt as desired, or try one or more of the following ideas:

   ✳ Outline-stitch or echo-quilt around the Guardian Angel.

   ✳ Machine doodle in the background.

   ✳ Machine doodle the world.

   ✳ Quilt star designs (pattern on pullout page) in the background.

   ✳ Use metallic or shiny thread.

3. Add a hanging sleeve, bind the edges with double-fold bias binding, and add a label.

Jest Wish

Materials: *44"-wide fabric*

½ yd. total assorted dark blue prints for stars
⅓ yd. gold print for star and moon
¼ yd. total assorted medium blue prints for stars
½ yd. blue print for inner and outer borders
¾ yd. dark blue print for middle border and Prairie Points
¼ yd. multicolored check for middle border
Scraps of bright prints for jester
Scraps of muslin for face and hands

⅞ yd. for backing
30" x 30" piece of batting
Gold bugle beads, size 9mm, for fishing rod and line
Silver seed beads, size 6/0, for fishing rod
9 gold jingle bells, size 10mm, for jester's hat and collar
9 gold jingle bells, size 15mm, for bottom border

Cutting

Use the patterns on page 63. Cut and prepare all appliqué shapes (moon, hat, collar, face, hand, sleeve, pants, legs, and shoes) from the appropriate fabrics, using your favorite appliqué method (pages 6–7). Rotary cut the remaining pieces listed below.

From the assorted dark blue prints, cut:
  9 strips, each 1½" x 42"; crosscut 224 squares, each 1½" x 1½", for background stars

From the gold print, cut:
  1 square, 1½" x 1½", for star center
  1 rectangle, 1" x 9"; crosscut 8 squares, each 1" x 1", for star points

From the medium blue prints, cut:
  5 strips, each 1" x 42"; crosscut 192 squares, each 1" x 1", for star points

From the blue print, cut:
  2 strips, each 1" x 42"; crosscut 2 strips, each 1" x 15½", and 2 strips, each 1" x 16½", for inner border
  4 strips, each 3½" x 27½", for outer border

From a dark blue print, cut:
  7 strips, each 2½" x 42"'; crosscut 104 squares, each 2½" x 2½", for middle border and large Prairie Points
  2 strips, 1¾" x 42"; crosscut 32 squares, each 1¾" x 1¾", for small Prairie Points

From the multicolored check, cut:
  4 strips, each 1½" x 42"; crosscut 32 rectangles, each 1½" x 4½", for middle border

Background

1. Using 96 assorted dark blue squares and the 192 medium blue squares, quick-piece 2 adjacent corners of each square. (Refer to "Quick Corners" on page 10.)

Make 96.

2. Using 4 assorted dark blue squares and 8 gold squares, quick-piece 2 adjacent corners of each square.

Make 4.

3. Assemble 24 blue stars and 1 gold star as shown. Press the seams in the direction indicated.

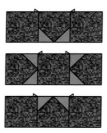 

Make 24 blue stars.
Make 1 gold star.

4. Arrange the star blocks as shown and sew them together to form 5 rows. Press the seams in opposite directions from row to row. Join the rows to form the background.

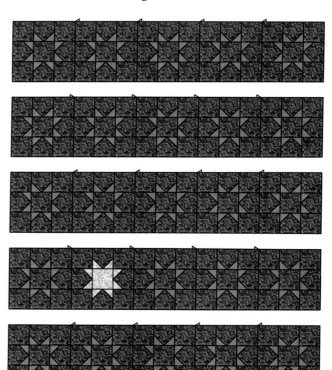

Borders

1. Sew the 1" x 15½" medium blue strips to the top and bottom edges of the quilt top, matching the center of the quilt top to the center of the border. Press all seams toward the inner border. Add the 1" x 16½" strips to opposite side edges of the quilt top in the same manner.

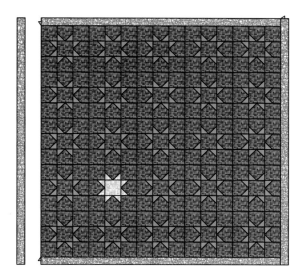

2. To create the middle diamond border, use 64 dark blue squares, each 2½" x 2½", and 32 multicolored rectangles, each 1½" x 4½".

3. Place a 2½" dark blue square in one corner of a multicolored rectangle, right sides together. Draw a line on the square from the corner of the square to the corner of the rectangle as shown. Sew on the line. Trim the excess dark blue print, leaving a ¼"-wide seam allowance. Fold and press the triangle to the corner of the rectangle. Corner edges will not match.

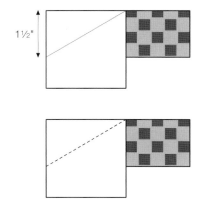

4. Repeat step 3, placing a dark blue square in the opposite corner.

5. Repeat steps 3 and 4 on all remaining rectangles.

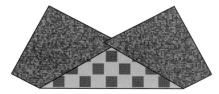

Make 32.

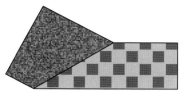

Make 32.

6. Turn the rectangles to the wrong side. Trim the excess fabric to match the rectangles.

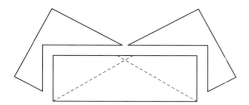

7. Sew rectangles together in pairs as shown to create 16 diamonds.

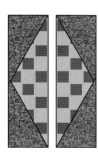

Make 16.

8. Join 4 diamonds end to end as shown for the borders. Add a 2½" x 2½" dark blue square to each end of 2 borders for the sides.

Top and Bottom Borders
Make 2.

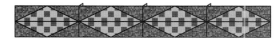

Side Borders
Make 2.

9. Sew the top and bottom borders to the quilt top. Add the side borders to opposite side edges, matching the seams. Press all seams toward the inner border.

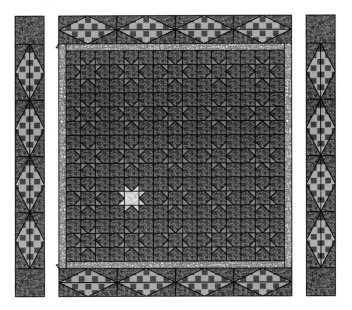

10. Following the directions for "Borders with Mitered Corners" on page 56, add a 3½" x 27½" blue print strip to each side of the quilt top, matching the center of the strip to the center of the quilt top. Miter the corners.

11. Press, trim, and square the edges of the quilt top to 26½" x 26½".

Appliqué

1. Before appliquéing the face to the background, trace the facial features onto the right side of the fabric, using a permanent fabric marker.

2. Referring to the appliqué plan, position and appliqué each piece in numerical order.

Finishing

Refer to "Finishing Techniques" on pages 57–60.

1. Layer the quilt top with batting and backing; baste.

2. Quilt as desired to within 1" of the border edges, or try one or more of the following ideas:
   * Outline-stitch or echo-quilt around the jester.
   * Machine doodle or quilt wavy lines in the background.
   * Quilt star designs in the borders.
   * Use metallic or shiny thread.

3. Trim the backing and batting even with the edges of the quilt top.

4. Fold each remaining 2½" dark blue square in half diagonally, wrong sides together; press.

5. Fold the resulting triangle in half as shown to form a smaller triangle with folds on 2 sides. Press the folds. Repeat with the 1¾" squares.

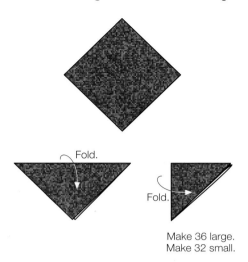

Make 36 large.
Make 32 small.

6. Arrange the large Prairie Points in the center of each side and on each corner of the quilt top as shown. The raw edges of the Prairie Points should be even with the outside edges of the quilt top.

7. Arrange the remaining Prairie Points evenly along each side of the quilt top, alternating small and large Prairie Points. All folds should point in the same direction. Each point should slip inside the opening of the one before it. Each side will have 9 large points and 8 small points. Pin in place.

8. Fold the backing and batting out of the way, then sew around each edge of the quilt top, using a ¼"-wide seam allowance. Pivot at each corner between the large Prairie Points.

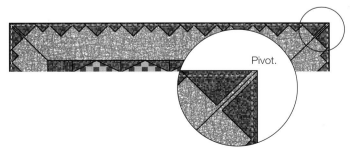

9. Turn the points toward the outer edge and press. Trim the batting even with the edge of the turned seam. Fold under ¼" along each edge of the backing and blindstitch in place, making sure your stitches do not show on the front. Clip the seam to the stitching line at the corner.

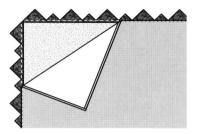

10. Add a hanging sleeve to the back of your quilt and add a label. Add a bell to the tip of each large Prairie Point along the bottom edge. Referring to the photograph on page 14, add bugle beads and seed beads to create the fishing pole and line.

Earth Angel

Color photo on page 20

Materials: *44"-wide fabric*

½ yd. yellow variegated or hand-dyed fabric for background

⅛ yd. blue print for piped border

⅝ yd. brown print for outer border and binding

¼ yd. total assorted green prints for hair, robe, wing, leaves, and vines

Scraps of blue, pink, and tan prints for flowers, face, feet, and hand

⅝ yd. for backing

21" x 28" piece of batting

Cutting

Use the patterns on pages 64–65. Cut and prepare all appliqué shapes (face, hand, feet, leaves, robe, wing, and flowers) from the appropriate fabrics, using your favorite appliqué method (pages 6–7). Rotary cut the remaining pieces listed below.

From the yellow fabric, cut:
 1 piece, 13½" x 19½", for background
From the blue print, cut:
 2 strips, each 1" x 42", for piping
From the brown print, cut:
 1 rectangle, 2½" x 17½", for bottom outer border
 1 piece, 15" x 15", for binding

Borders

1. Fold the 13½" x 19½" piece of background fabric in half lengthwise.
2. Place the inner arch template (on pullout page) even with the fold and the upper and side edges; cut along the curve through both layers. Open the background piece and press flat.

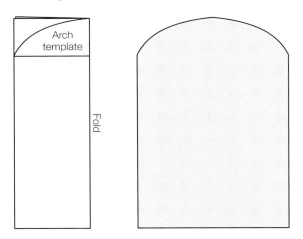

3. Sew the 2 blue print strips together end to end. Fold the strip in half, wrong sides together, and press along the fold. From the folded strip, cut 1 strip 13½" long, and 1 strip 51" long, for the piped border.

4. Keeping the raw edges even, sew the 13½"-long piping strip to the bottom edge of the background. Press flat.

5. Beginning at the bottom edge and keeping the raw edges even, pin the 51"-long piping strip to the sides and top of the background. Clip curves as shown. Sew the piping to the background, easing it at the corners and on the curve; trim even with the bottom border. Press flat.

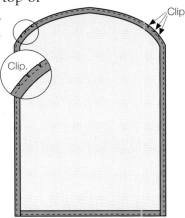

6. Using the outer arch template on the pullout page, cut an arch from the brown print.
7. Mark the center of the yellow background piece and the center of the arch at the top of the curve. With right sides together, match the centers and pin the border to the background, beginning at the center. Clip the border as shown to help ease it around the curve. Sew the border to the background, easing around the corners and being careful not to stretch the outer edge of the border. Press the seam toward the border. Trim the bottom of the border even with the background.

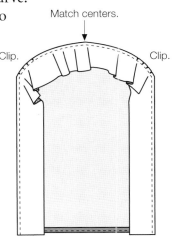

8. Sew the 2½" x 17½" piece of brown print to the center section along the bottom edge. Press toward the bottom border.

Appliqué

1. Before appliquéing the face to the background, trace the facial features onto the right side of the fabric, using a permanent fabric marker.
2. I used a ¼" bias-bar tool to create the vines for the Earth Angel. Cut ⅞"-wide bias strips of green print. You will need 1 piece about 24" long and 1 piece about 30" long. Fold the pieces in half, wrong sides together. Using a ⅛"-wide seam allowance, sew along the long edge. Insert the ¼" bias bar into one end of the tube. Adjust the tube so the seam is in the center of the flat side. Steam-press on both sides. Push the bar through until the whole tube is pressed.

⅛" seam ───▸

Fold

Bias bar ───▸

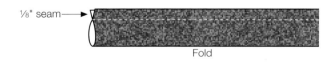

3. Referring to the appliqué plan, position and appliqué the vines in place. Add the remaining pieces in numerical order.

Finishing

Refer to "Finishing Techniques" on pages 57–60.
1. Layer the quilt top with batting and backing; baste.
2. Quilt as desired, or try one or more of the following ideas:
    * Outline-stitch or echo-quilt around the Earth Angel.
    * Machine doodle or quilt horizontal lines in the background.
    * Quilt leaf designs in the robe and wing.
    * Quilt diagonal lines in the outer border.
    * Use metallic or shiny thread.
3. Add a hanging sleeve, bind the edges with double-fold bias binding, and add a label.

Star-Spangled Salute

Quilt Size: 32" x 42"

Color photo on page 16

Materials: *44"-wide fabric*

¾ yd. blue print for stars, flag, inner border, hat brim, and jacket

¾ yd. red stripe for triangles, pants, and hat

¼ yd. gold print for stars, beard, and hair

⅛ yd. red print #1 for flag and shoes

⅛ yd. white print for stripes

⅜ yd. light print for background

1 yd. red print #2 for outer border and binding

Scrap of blue print for vest

Scraps of muslin for face and hands

1⅜ yds. for backing

36" x 46" piece of batting

Cutting

Use the patterns on page 66 and on the pullout page. Cut and prepare all appliqué shapes (hat, face, hands, beard, vest, jacket, pants, cuff, and stars) from the appropriate fabrics, using your favorite appliqué method (pages 6–7). Rotary cut the remaining pieces listed below.

From the blue print, cut:
4 squares, each 7" x 7"; cut each square once diagonally for a total of 8 triangles

Make 8.

8 squares, each 2" x 2", for flag
4 strips, each 2½" x 42"; crosscut 2 strips, each 2½" x 24½", and 2 strips, each 2½" x 34", for inner border
4 squares, each 2½" x 2½", for outer border corner squares

From the red stripe, cut:
4 squares, each 7" x 7"; cut the squares on the bias of the fabric as shown below, then cut each square once diagonally for 8 triangles
1 rectangle, 5" x 17", cut from the lengthwise grain, for pants (piece 2)

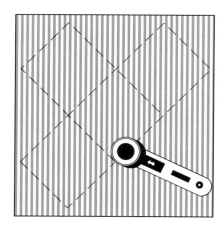

Cut 8 triangles.

From the gold print, cut:
1 square, 2" x 2", for pieced star
8 squares, each 1½" x 1½", for pieced star points

From red print #1, cut:
2 strips, each 1¼" x 42"; crosscut 3 strips, each 1¼" x 8", and 4 strips, each 1¼" x 12½", for flag

From the white print, cut:
2 strips, each 1¼" x 42"; crosscut 3 strips, each 1¼" x 8", and 3 strips, each 1¼" x 12½".

From the light print, cut:
1 rectangle, 12½" x 34", for background

From red print #2, cut:
4 strips, each 2½" x 42"; from the strips, cut:
2 strips, each 2½" x 28½", for outer border;
2 strips, each 2½" x 38", for outer border;
4 squares, each 2½" x 2½", for inner border corner squares
1 square, 20" x 20", for binding

Background

1. Sew a blue print triangle to each red stripe triangle to make 8 half-square triangle units. Press the seams toward the blue triangle. Trim each unit to 6½" x 6½".

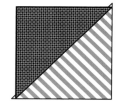

Make 8.

2. Arrange the half-square triangle units into 4 rows of 2 units each as shown. Sew the units together in rows; press the seams in opposite directions from row to row. Sew the rows together.

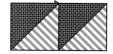

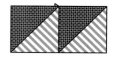

3. To make the star for the flag, sew a gold 1½" square to each of 2 adjacent corners of 4 blue print 2" squares. (See "Quick Corners" on page 10.)

Make 4.

4. Arrange the remaining 4 blue print 2" squares, the gold 2" square, and the pieced squares from step 3 to form a star as shown. Sew the squares together in rows. Press the seams in the direction of the arrows. Sew the rows together.

5. Arrange the red print #1 and white 1¼" x 8" strips as shown. Sew the strips together and press all seams toward the red strips.

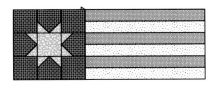

6. Join the pieced star block to the left side of the striped section with the red stripe at the top. Press the seam toward the star.

7. Arrange the red print #1 and white 1¼" x 12½" strips as shown and sew them together. Begin and end with a red strip. Press all seams toward the red.

8. Join the star and striped section of the flag to the lower striped section along the long edge as shown. Press the seam toward the red stripe.

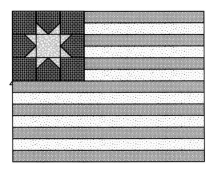

9. Add the flag to the upper edge of the triangle section as shown. Press the seam toward the flag.

10. Join the background piece to the left side of the flag section along the long edge. Press the seam toward the background piece.

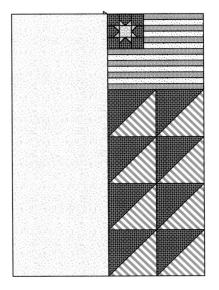

Borders

1. Sew the 2½" x 24½" strips of blue print to the top and bottom edges of the quilt top, matching the center of the border strips to the center of the quilt-top edges. Press these seams and all remaining seams toward the border strips.

2. Join 2½" squares of red print #2 to each end of the remaining blue print strips. Sew these strips to opposite sides of the quilt top, matching the seams.

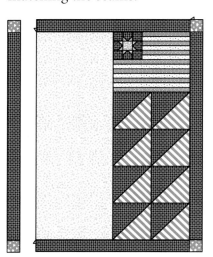

Make 2.

3. Sew the 2½" x 28½" strips of red print #2 to the top and bottom edges of the quilt top.

4. Join a blue print 2½" square to each end of the 2½" x 38" red print #2 strips. Press the seam toward the border. Sew these strips to opposite sides of the quilt top.

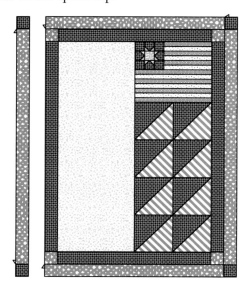

Appliqué

1. Referring to the quilt plan on page 39, position and appliqué a flag star on each blue print triangle, and a corner star to each inner corner square.

2. Before appliquéing the face to the background, trace the facial features onto the right side of the fabric, using a permanent fabric marker.

3. Referring to the appliqué plan at right, position and appliqué each piece to the background in numerical order.

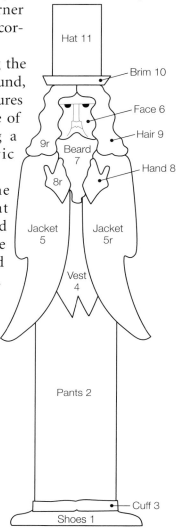

Finishing

Refer to "Finishing Techniques" on pages 57–60.

1. Layer the quilt top with batting and backing; baste.

2. Quilt as desired, or try one or more of the following ideas:
   * Stipple-quilt around the stars.
   * Echo-quilt around the stars.
   * Quilt wavy lines in the borders.

3. Add a hanging sleeve, bind the edges with double-fold bias binding, and add a label.

Fairy Garden

Color photo on page 15

Materials: *44"-wide fabric*

⅞ yd. blue gradated solid for background

½ yd. total assorted green prints for border, stalks, stems, and leaves

⅜ yd. floral print for ground and border

1½ yds. purple print for border and binding

⅜ yd. assorted yellow prints for Prairie Points

¼ yd. each of 3 prints for hollyhock Yo-yos

8 assorted squares, each 10" x 10", for fairy, mushroom, and bugs

¼ yd. assorted brown prints for sunflower centers and bug bottom

1½ yds. for backing

39" x 53" piece of batting

Cutting

Use the patterns on the pullout page. Cut and prepare all appliqué shapes(fairy, leaf, mushroom, and bug) from the appropriate fabrics, using your favorite appliqué method (pages 6–7). Rotary cut the remaining pieces listed below.

From the blue solid, cut:
    1 rectangle, 22" x 39½", for background
    2 strips, each 2" x 39½", for background
    1 strip, 1¼" x 39½", for background

From 1 green print, cut:
    4 strips, each 2" x 42", for four-patch units

From the assorted green prints, cut:
    3 strips total, each 1¼" x 39½", for stalks

From the floral print, cut:
    4 strips, each 2" x 42", for four-patch units
    1 strip, 1½" x 27½", for ground

From the purple print, cut:
    3 strips, each 5½" x 42"; crosscut 16 squares, each 5½" x 5½"; cut each square twice diagonally for 64 edge setting triangles for border

    1 strip, 4¾" x 42"; crosscut 2 squares, each 4¾" x 4¾", for border corners. Trim the remainder of the strip to 3" wide, then cut 4 squares, each 3" x 3"; cut each square once diagonally for 8 corner setting triangles for border

    1 square, 23" x 23", for binding

From the assorted yellow prints, cut:
    40 squares (total), each 3" x 3", for sunflower Prairie Points

Background

1. Arrange the 1¼"-wide stalk pieces and the 1¼"- and 2"-wide background strips as shown. Sew them together; press seams toward the stalks.

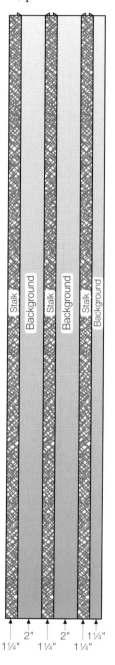

2. Join the stalk unit to the right edge of the 22" x 39½" background piece. Press the seam toward the stalk unit. Add the 1½" x 27½" floral strip to the bottom edge of the background section to form the ground. Press the seam toward the background.

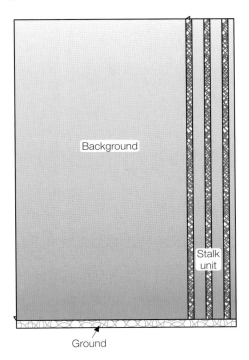

Background

Stalk unit

Ground

Pieced Border

1. Sew each green 2" x 42" strip to a floral 2" x 42" strip to make 4 strip units. Press the seam toward the floral strip in each unit.
2. Crosscut a total of 68 segments, each 2" wide, from the strip units.

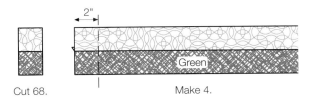

2"

Green

Cut 68.

Make 4.

3. Sew pairs of segments together as shown to make 34 four-patch units.

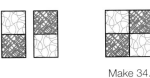

Make 34.

4. Sew a purple edge setting triangle to 2 opposite edges of 28 four-patch units to create 28 diagonal rows. Press the seams toward the triangle.

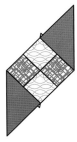

Make 28.

5. Sew purple edge setting triangles to adjacent edges of 2 four-patch units to create 2 triangle units. Press the seams toward the triangles.

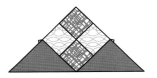

Triangle Unit
Make 2.

6. Arrange the 4 remaining four-patch units together with purple edge and corner setting triangles as shown; sew them together to make 4 row-end units. Press the seams toward the triangles.

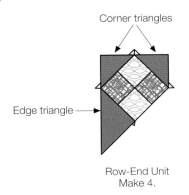

Corner triangles

Edge triangle

Row-End Unit
Make 4.

7. Arrange 5 diagonal rows for the top and bottom borders, and 9 rows for each side border. Add the triangle units, end units, and squares as shown. Sew them together; press the seams to one side.

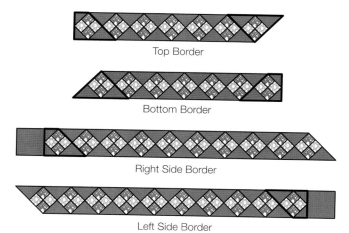

Top Border

Bottom Border

Right Side Border

Left Side Border

8. Sew the top and the bottom borders to the top and bottom edges of the quilt top as shown. Begin sewing at the straight edge and end the stitching ¼" from the diagonal edge. Press the seams toward the center. Sew the side borders to opposite sides of the quilt top in the same manner, matching the seams.

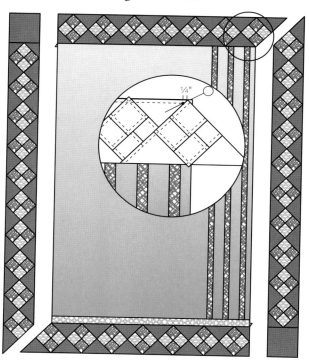

9. Pin the diagonal border corners together to create a mitered corner. (See "Borders with Mitered Corners" on page 56.) Stitch them from the outer corner to the inner corner.

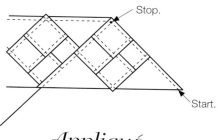

Stop.

Start.

Appliqué

1. To make the sunflower Prairie Points, fold each yellow 3" square in half diagonally, wrong sides together, and press the fold. Fold the resulting triangle in half again to form a smaller triangle; press the folds.

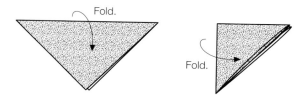

Fold.

Fold.

2. Referring to the quilt plan on page 43, position the sunflower centers on the stalks. Arrange the Prairie Points around the sunflower centers, covering the raw edges of the Prairie Points; pin in place. Machine stitch through all layers.

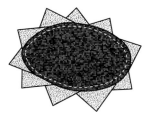

3. Before appliquéing the fairy and bugs to the background, trace the facial features onto the right side of the fabric, using a permanent fabric marker.

4. Referring to the appliqué plan below and the quilt plan, position and appliqué each piece.

5. Make circle templates. Trace around them on the wrong side of each of 3 prints for the hollyhock Yo-yos. Cut 3 circles 6" in diameter, 5 circles 4" in diameter, and 5 circles 3½" in diameter from *each* fabric. You'll have a few extras you can either add to the quilt or save for another project.

6. Turn under a scant ¼"-wide seam allowance. Using double thread, sew a running stitch around the edge of each circle. Draw up the thread and pull it tight to shape a Yo-yo; knot the thread.

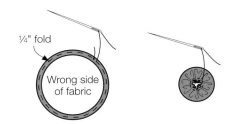

7. Referring to the quilt plan, position the Yo-yos, gathered side up, along the stalks to represent hollyhock flowers. Tack them in place by hand or by machine, using several short zigzag stitches. Add hollyhock leaves and appliqué in place.

Finishing

Refer to "Finishing Techniques" on pages 57–60.

1. Layer the quilt top with batting and backing; baste.

2. Quilt as desired, or try one or more of the following ideas:
   * Quilt a fairy wand, a firefly, and a dragonfly (patterns on pullout page) in the background.
   * Use metallic thread.
   * Quilt parallel rows in the background, using invisible thread.

3. Add a hanging sleeve, bind the edges with double-fold bias binding, and add a label.

Fred A. Scarecrow

Quilt Size: 33" x 51"

Color photo on page 17

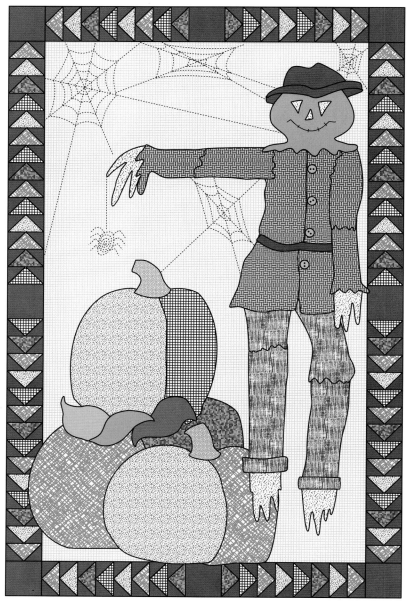

Materials: *44"-wide fabric*

1⅜ yds. tan check for background
1¼ yds. total assorted orange prints for flying-
   geese units and pumpkins
1½ yds. total assorted black prints for flying-geese
   units, hat, and binding
½ yd. plaid for shirt
⅜ yd. blue print for pants and cuffs
¼ yd. tan print for hands and feet

¼ yd. brown solid for face
Assorted scraps of brown print for stems
⅛ yd. green print for leaves
1⅝ yds. for backing
37" x 55" piece of batting
4 orange buttons, ¾" diameter
1 yd. twine for scarecrow

Cutting

Use the patterns on pages 67–75 and on the pullout page. Cut and prepare all appliqué pieces, using your favorite appliqué method (pages 6–7). Rotary cut the remaining pieces listed below.

From the tan check, cut:
  1 rectangle, 27½" x 45½", for background
From the assorted orange prints, cut:
  5 strips, each 3½" x 42"; crosscut 88 rectangles, each 2" x 3½", for flying-geese units
From the assorted black prints, cut:
  9 strips, each 2" x 42"; crosscut 176 squares, each 2" x 2", for flying-geese units
  1 strip, 3½" x 42"; crosscut 8 squares, each 3½" x 3½", for border squares
  1 piece, 24" x 24", for binding

Flying Geese Border

1. Using 88 orange 2" x 3½" rectangles and 176 black 2" squares, make 88 flying-geese units. (See "Quick Flying Geese" on page 10.)

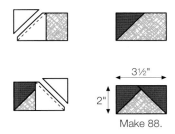

Make 88.

2. Arrange 8 flying-geese units as shown and sew them together for the top and bottom borders. Press the seams in the direction of the arrows. Make 4 sets. Join pairs of sets with a black 3½" square in the center as shown. Press the seams toward the black square. Make 2 borders.

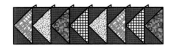

Make 4.

Top and Bottom Borders
Make 2.

3. Arrange 14 flying-geese units as shown and sew them together for the side borders. Press the seams in the direction of the arrows. Make 4 sets. Join pairs of sets with a black 3½" square in the center as shown. Press the seams toward the black square. Add a black 3½" square to each short end of each border unit. Make 2 borders.

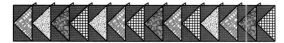

Make 4.

Side Borders
Make 2.

4. Sew the top and bottom borders to the top and bottom edges of the background rectangle. Press the seams toward the background. Add the side borders to opposite sides of the background rectangle, matching the seams. Press the seams toward the background.

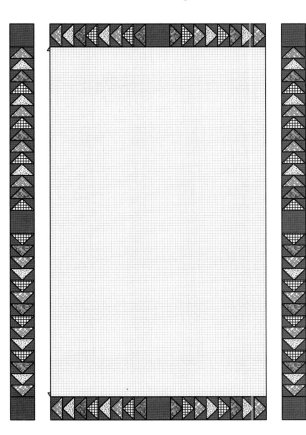

Appliqué

1. Before appliquéing the face to the background, trace the facial features onto the right side of the fabric, using a permanent fabric marker. You may prefer to appliqué the eyes and nose and embroider the mouth.

2. Referring to the appliqué plan, position and appliqué each piece in numerical order. Use a buttonhole stitch if you prefer a more country look. Allow some of the pumpkins to extend into the border.

3. Cut the twine to the correct size for a belt and to go around the sleeves and neck. Use a large X stitch to hold the twine in place.

Twine

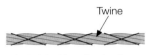

X stitch holds twine in place.

Finishing

Refer to "Finishing Techniques" on pages 57–60.

1. Layer the quilt top with batting and backing; baste.

2. Quilt as desired, or try one or more of the following ideas:
    * Stitch a 2" grid across the background.
    * Add ridges on the pumpkins and leaves.
    * Quilt spirals for the vines and through the centers of the flying-geese units.

3. Add a hanging sleeve, bind the edges with double-fold bias binding, and add a label.

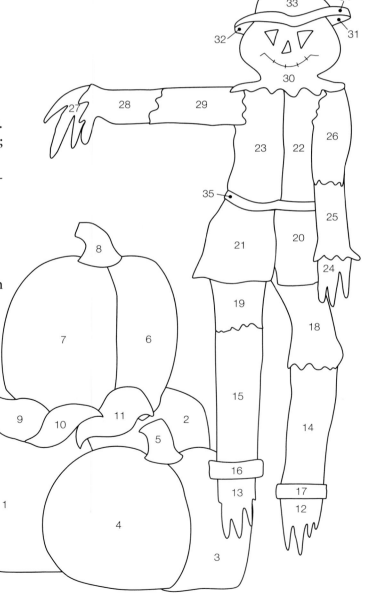

Fred A. Scarecrow

Hello Santa!

Quilt Size: 22" x 32"

Color photo on page 18

Materials: *44"-wide fabric*

⅝ yd. blue-gray solid for background

⅜ yd. red print for Santa's clothes

⅛ yd. white print #1 for Santa's cuffs

8" x 10" white print #2 for Santa's beard,
  moustache, and eyebrows

¼ yd. black print #1 for Santa's boot and mittens

6" x 7" muslin for Santa's face

¼ yd. total assorted green prints for Santa's pack

4" x 8" black print #2 for chimney rim

¼ yd. total assorted gray prints for chimney

¼ yd. holiday print for checkerboard border

¼ yd. green solid for checkerboard border

¾ yd. for backing

26" x 36" piece of batting

½ yd. for binding

50 buttons, ⅝" diameter (optional)

25 assorted small toy ornaments

Cutting

Use the patterns on pages 76–77 and on the pullout page. Cut and prepare all appliqué shapes from the appropriate fabrics, using your favorite appliqué method (pages 6–7). Rotary cut the remaining pieces listed below.

From the blue-gray solid, cut:
    1 rectangle, 12½" x 18½", for background
    1 rectangle, 12½" x 16½", for background
From black print #2, cut:
    1 strip, 2½" x 6½", for chimney rim
From *each* of the assorted gray prints, cut:
    1 strip, each 2½" wide
From the holiday print, cut:
    4 strips, each 1½" x 42"
From the green solid, cut:
    4 strips, each 1½" x 42"
    1 square, 18" x 18", for binding

Background

1. From the assorted 2½"-wide gray strips, cut pieces in random lengths ranging from 1" to 5½" long. Sew the pieces together to make a total of 7 units, each 2½" x 6½".

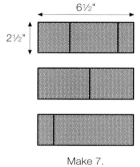

6½"

2½"

Make 7.

2. Arrange the units as desired and sew them together to make the chimney. Add the black 2½" x 6½" strip to the top edge for the rim. Press the seams in the direction of the arrows.

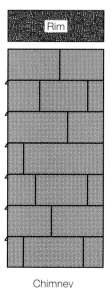

Rim

Chimney

3. Sew the chimney to the long edge of the 12½" x 16½" piece of background fabric as shown. Press the seam toward the background.

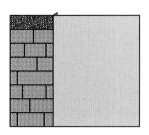

4. Add the remaining background piece to the top edge and press the seam toward the background.

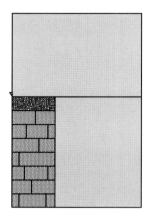

Pieced Border

1. Sew each green 1½" x 42" strip to a holiday print 1½" x 42" strip to make 4 strip units. Press the seam toward the print strip in each unit.
2. Cut a total of 100 segments, each 1½" wide, from the strip units.

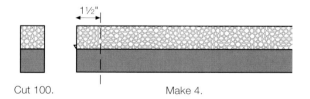

1½"

Cut 100.   Make 4.

3. Sew pairs of segments together as shown to make 50 four-patch units. Press the seams to one side.

Make 50.

4. Arrange 16 four-patch units as shown and sew them together for each side border. Arrange 9 four-patch units for the top and bottom borders. Press the seams to one side.

Side Borders
Make 2.

Top and Bottom Borders
Make 2.

5. Sew the top and bottom borders to the top and bottom edges of the quilt top; press the seams toward the quilt top. Add the side borders to opposite sides of the quilt top; press the seams toward the quilt top.

Appliqué

1. Before appliquéing the face to the background, trace the facial features onto the right side of the fabric, using a permanent fabric marker, or embroider.
2. Referring to the appliqué plan, position and appliqué each piece in numerical order.

Finishing

Refer to "Finishing Techniques" on pages 57–60.
1. Layer the quilt top with batting and backing; baste.

2. Quilt as desired, or try one or more of the following ideas:
   * Outline- or echo-stitch around Santa and the bricks.
   * Quilt spiral doodles in the borders.
   * Stitch small snowflake designs (pattern on pullout page) in the background.
   * Quilt snow on the chimney rim.
3. Add a hanging sleeve, bind the edges with double-fold bias binding, and add a label.

Creative Option

Use your finished quilt for a Christmas countdown. Attach 25 buttons randomly along the bottom and up the right and left edges of the quilt. Hang small ornaments or toys from each button. Sew an additional 25 buttons on and above Santa's pack. Keep track of the days until Christmas by moving the ornaments from the outer edges of the quilt to the buttons on Santa's pack.

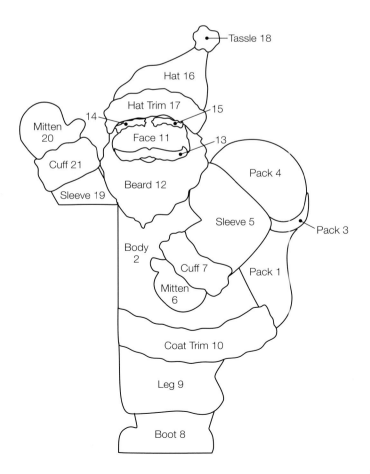

Quilt Top Assembly

Squaring Up Blocks

When your pieced blocks are complete, take the time to square them up. Use a Bias Square ruler to measure the blocks. Each block should be the finished size plus ½" (¼" seam allowance on all sides). For example, if the finished size is 3", square up the block to 3½".

Make sure to trim all sides of the blocks equally, placing the diagonal line of the ruler through the center of the block.

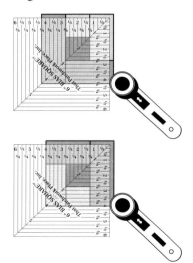

Adding Borders

It is important that borders on opposite sides of the quilt be of equal length. If the sides do not measure the same, the quilt will hang unevenly, and the borders and edges will be wavy. Follow the directions below to ensure the borders are even.

Borders with Straight-Cut Corners

1. Measure the quilt top lengthwise through the center and cut two border strips to that length.

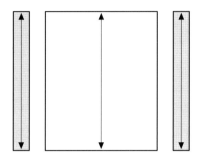

2. Fold both border strips in half crosswise to find the center; mark each strip with a pin. Find the center of each side of the quilt top by folding it in half; mark each side with a pin.

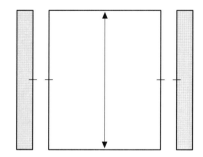

3. With right sides together, match the center of the side border strip to the center of the side edge; pin. Match the ends; pin. Pin the remainder of the border to the quilt top, easing as necessary.

4. Stitch the borders to the quilt top; press the seam allowances toward the borders.

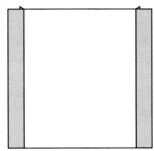

5. Repeat steps 1–4 for the top and bottom borders, this time measuring the quilt top crosswise through the center, and including the side borders.

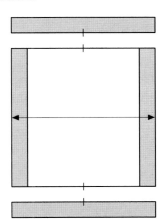

Borders with Corner Squares

1. Measure and cut the strips for all four sides before you sew any borders to the quilt top.

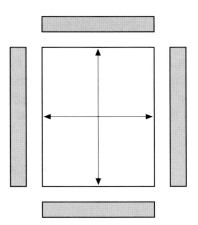

2. Mark, pin, and sew the side borders to opposite sides of the quilt top. Press the seams toward the borders.

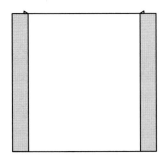

3. Add corner squares to both ends of the top and bottom borders, pressing the seams toward the borders. Match the centers and seams; pin, then sew the borders to the quilt top.

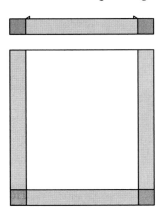

Borders with Mitered Corners

1. Measure the quilt top through the center, both lengthwise and crosswise. Measure the width of the border. To determine how long to cut the side border strips, add the lengthwise measurement of the quilt top, the width of the border times 2, plus 4". To determine how long to cut the top and bottom border strips, add the crosswise measurement of the quilt top, the width of the border times 2, plus 4".

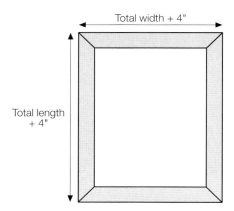

Total width + 4"

Total length + 4"

2. Fold each border section in half crosswise to find the center; mark each with a pin. Repeat with the quilt top. With right sides together, match the center of the border to the center of the side edge; pin together along the edges.

3. Stitch each border to the quilt top, using a ¼"-wide seam allowance. Start and stop your stitching ¼" from the corners of the quilt top. The border strips should extend the same distance at each end of the quilt. Press the seams toward the borders.

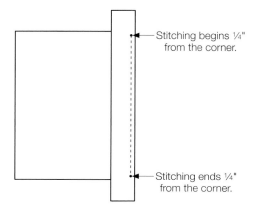

Stitching begins ¼" from the corner.

Stitching ends ¼" from the corner.

4. Fold the quilt diagonally, right sides together. Align the edges of the borders, then pin them together.

5. Using a ruler with a 45° angle, align the horizontal lines on the ruler with the stitching lines on the border. Draw a line on the wrong side of the border strip, beginning at the stitching on the quilt corner and extending it to the outside edge of the border.

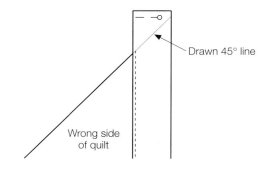

Drawn 45° line

Wrong side of quilt

6. Stitch on the marked line, sewing from the quilt corner to the outside edge of the border. Trim the seam to ¼"; press open.

Finishing Techniques

Transferring Quilting Designs

There are several ways to transfer quilting designs to your quilt top. First, photocopy the design you wish to use, enlarging or reducing it to the correct size as necessary. Then use one of the following methods to mark your quilt top:

Use a light box. You may use a home-made device, such as a piece of glass between two halves of a table with a lamp underneath, or you may use a commercial light box. Tape the copied design on the glass. Place the quilt top over the design. Trace the design onto the quilt top using a mechanical pencil, No. 3 pencil, or marker.

Create a stencil. Using the copied design, trace and cut a stencil from heavy Mylar. More intricate designs may prove difficult. Remember to leave "bridges" between cutouts, or the whole thing will fall apart. Using a pencil or marker, mark the quilt top.

Use Con-Tact® paper. Trace shapes or templates onto the plastic adhesive and cut them out. Peel away the backing and stick the template to the quilt top. Quilt around the shape(s), then peel them off and reposition them on the quilt in another place. Cut several templates at one time. When the sticky stuff is gone, use a new template. No marking is necessary.

Choosing Batting and Backing

A large variety of battings is now available. Each lends a different look and feel to a quilted piece. I used either 100% cotton or 80% cotton/20% polyester batting for all the designs in this book. These battings require slightly less basting because they don't shift a lot, and they are easier to machine quilt. I like to use cotton batting because, when washed, it shrinks, giving the quilt added dimension. If this is your first attempt at machine quilting, this can also help to hide less-than-perfect stitches. Quilting requirements differ from batting to batting, so check the package. It will include suggested quilting distances. Remember, too, that quilting "eats up" some of the length and width of your quilt (less of a problem with thin battings than thick), so your quilt may be slightly smaller after quilting. Cut the batting 2" to 4" larger than your quilt top on each side.

A solid-color backing fabric shows off quilting stitches best. If you prefer to disguise your quilting stitches, use a print or a busy floral for the backing. Cut the backing fabric 2" to 4" larger than your project.

Layering the Quilt

Carefully prepare the layers for quilting so your quilt is straight and wrinkle-free.
1. Fold the backing in half, matching the edges, and mark the center of each edge. Press the backing and lay it, wrong side up, on a table. Place pieces of masking tape about 6" apart to secure the backing to the table.
2. Lay the batting on top of the backing; match the center points and smooth out all the wrinkles.

3. Center the quilt top over the batting and backing. Smooth out the quilt top. Your quilt sandwich should be wrinkle-free and taut, but not distorted.

4. Baste all three layers together with long running stitches, or place 1" rustproof safety pins every 3" to 4". Do not place pins where you will be quilting. Beginning at the center, work your way out to the edges, basting both diagonals first, then basting in a grid as shown at right.

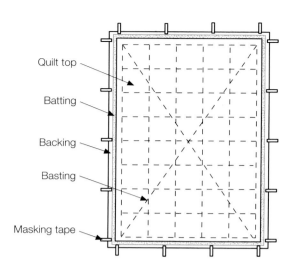

Quilt top
Batting
Backing
Basting
Masking tape

Machine Quilting

1. To machine quilt straight lines, use a walking or even-feed foot.

2. Quilt vertical, horizontal, or diagonal rows to anchor the layers. Starting in the center of one edge, quilt either a horizontal or vertical line, or start in a corner and quilt diagonally through the quilt. If possible, use sashings or blocks as a guide for anchoring the rows.

3. After the anchoring rows have been quilted, begin in the center and quilt your designs in blocks or rows. If there are no blocks or rows to follow, start with the center design and quilt toward the edges.

4. Stitch all the rows in a section in the same direction, working from edge to edge. Turn the quilt and repeat the process on the opposite side.

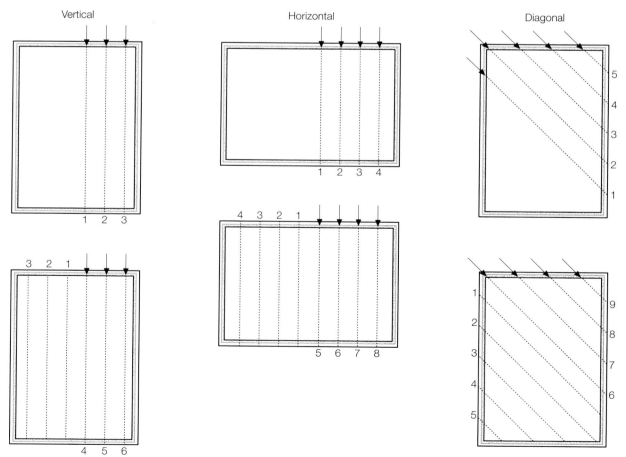

Finishing Techniques

5. Quilt the borders last. Begin from the center of the border, if possible, or start with a stabilizing curve or spine in the quilting design.

6. To add curves or to quilt designs that are not straight lines, drop or cover the feed dogs of your machine and use a darning foot. For more information on machine quilting, refer to *Machine Quilting Made Easy* by Maurine Noble (That Patchwork Place).

Adding a Sleeve

A hanging sleeve is necessary if you plan to display your finished project. Measure the top edge of your quilt. Cut a piece of fabric 6" wide and 2" narrower than your quilt top. Hem both short ends of the strip.

Fold the strip in half lengthwise. Center it along the top edge of the quilt; pin in place. The sleeve will be slightly narrower than the quilt top and should hang free. You will stitch it to the quilt when you sew on the binding.

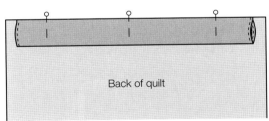

Back of quilt

To add a sleeve to a quilt with a curved top, measure the width of the quilt 2" from the top edge. Cut the sleeve 6" wide and as wide as the quilt. Hem the short edges as directed, then fold the strip in half lengthwise, wrong sides together, and stitch ¼" from the long edge. Fold the sleeve so the seam is in the center of the back; press. Place the sleeve about 2" down from the top center point and as close to the side edges as possible; stitch in place along both long edges.

Binding the Quilt

I prefer to use bias-cut bindings for my quilts because they wear better than straight-cut bindings.

1. To make a double-fold bias binding, cut a square of fabric the required size for your project. Trim the selvages, but mark the selvage edges of the fabric with a pin. Draw a diagonal line from corner to corner and cut the square in half on that line.

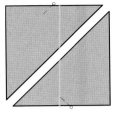

Mark top and bottom of square and divide it on the diagonal.

2. Place the triangles, right sides together, matching the pinned edges. Sew the triangles together with a ¼"-wide seam allowance along the pinned edges.

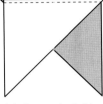

Join the marked sides.

3. Press the seam open. Mark lines 2¼" apart and parallel to the bias edges on the wrong side of the fabric. Place a pin ¼" from the edge at the first marked line on the right-hand side, and another pin at the top left corner.

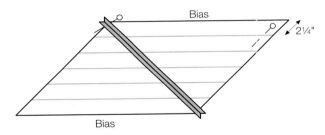

Bias

2¼"

Bias

4. Fold the piece right sides together, forming a tube. Match the pins and marked lines at the ¼" seam line; sew. Cut the tube apart on the marked lines.

Stitch ends together to form a cylinder, offsetting edges by width of one line.

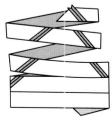

Cut along lines to form a continuous strip.

5. Fold the strip in half, wrong sides together, and press. Open the binding, turn it under ¼" at one end, and press. Refold the strip.

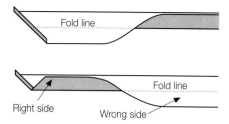

6. Trim any excess batting and backing so the edges are straight and all the corners are 90°. Use a rotary cutter and ruler to make this step go quickly and accurately.

7. Beginning in the middle of one side, sew the binding to the right side of the quilt, using a ¼"-wide seam allowance. Keep the raw edges of the binding even with the edge of the quilt. Be careful not to stretch the binding or the quilt. End the stitching ¼" from the corner; backstitch. Cut the thread and remove the quilt from the machine.

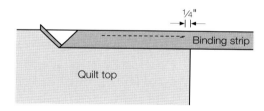

8. Fold the binding away from the quilt as shown, then fold it again so the binding is even with the next edge of the quilt; sew the next edge. Repeat with the remaining edges and corners.

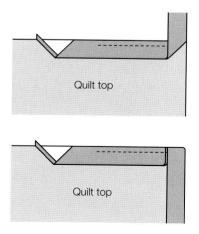

9. When you reach the beginning of the binding, overlap the first stitches by about 1". Trim any excess binding, cutting the end at a 45° angle. Tuck the end of the binding into the fold and finish the seam.

10. Turn the binding to the back and blindstitch in place. At each corner, stitch to the corner seam, then fold the binding to form a mitered corner on the back of the quilt.

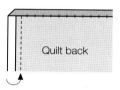

11. Carefully blindstitch the bottom edge of the hanging sleeve to the backing of the quilt, making sure the stitches don't show on the front.

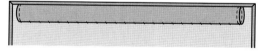

Blindstitch bottom edge of sleeve.

Signing the Quilt

Sign and date your quilt! You may wish to embroider or quilt your name and the date for future generations, or attach a fabric label to the back. The label should include your name, the date, the name or the meaning of the design, and why you made the quilt.

Templates

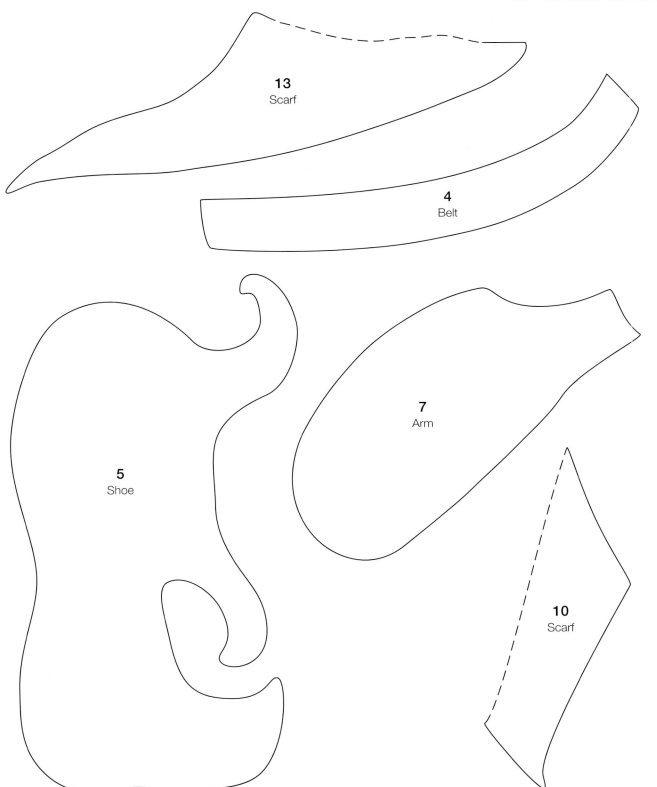

13
Scarf

4
Belt

5
Shoe

7
Arm

10
Scarf

Jack Frost
Appliqué Templates
Cut 1 each unless otherwise indicated.

11
Scarf

12
Scarf

9
Arm

3
Pouch

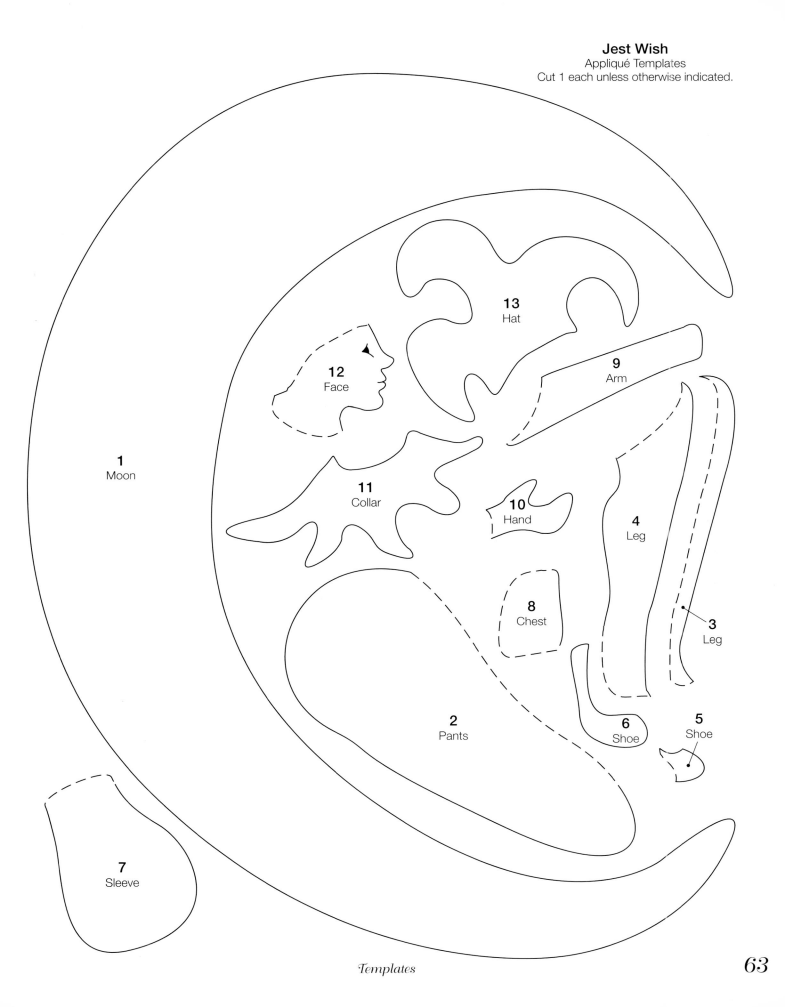

Jest Wish
Appliqué Templates
Cut 1 each unless otherwise indicated.

1
Moon

13
Hat

12
Face

9
Arm

11
Collar

10
Hand

4
Leg

3
Leg

8
Chest

2
Pants

6
Shoe

5
Shoe

7
Sleeve

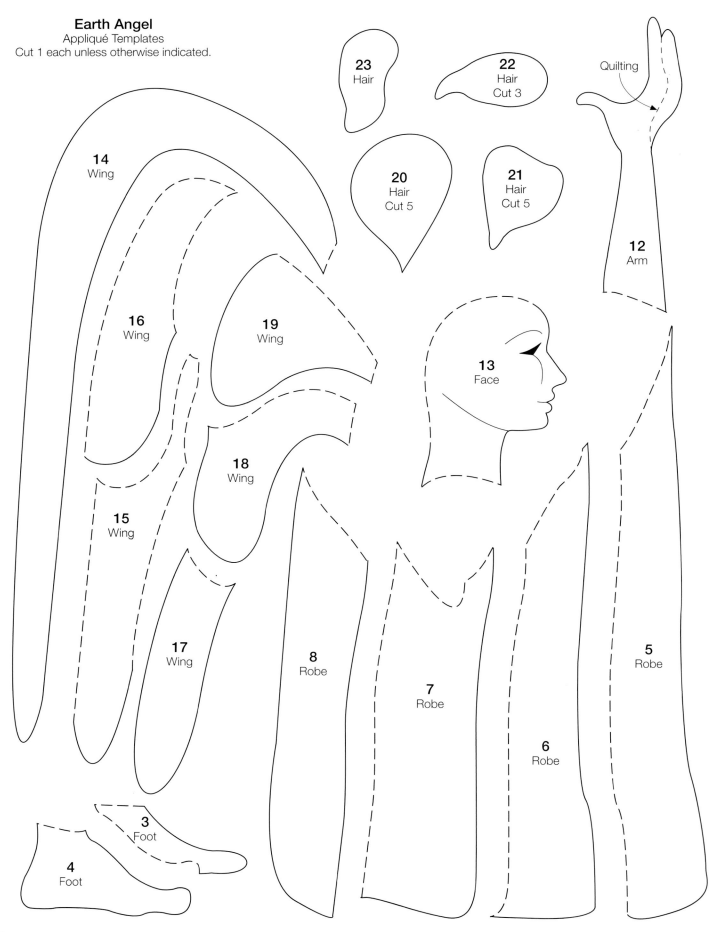

Earth Angel
Appliqué Templates
Cut 1 each unless otherwise indicated.

23
Hair

22
Hair
Cut 3

Quilting

14
Wing

20
Hair
Cut 5

21
Hair
Cut 5

12
Arm

16
Wing

19
Wing

13
Face

18
Wing

15
Wing

5
Robe

17
Wing

8
Robe

7
Robe

6
Robe

3
Foot

4
Foot

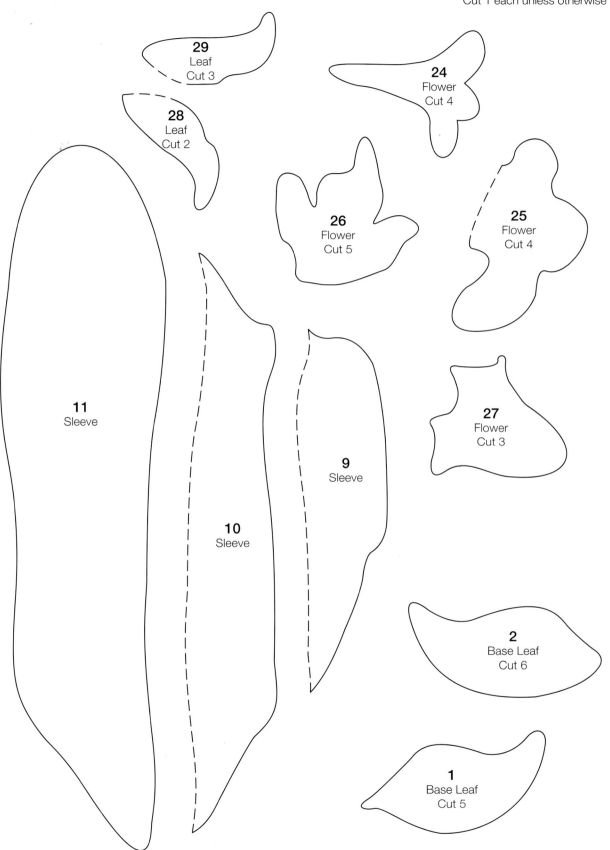

29
Leaf
Cut 3

24
Flower
Cut 4

28
Leaf
Cut 2

26
Flower
Cut 5

25
Flower
Cut 4

11
Sleeve

27
Flower
Cut 3

10
Sleeve

9
Sleeve

2
Base Leaf
Cut 6

1
Base Leaf
Cut 5

Star-Spangled Salute
Appliqué Templates
Cut 1 each unless otherwise indicated.

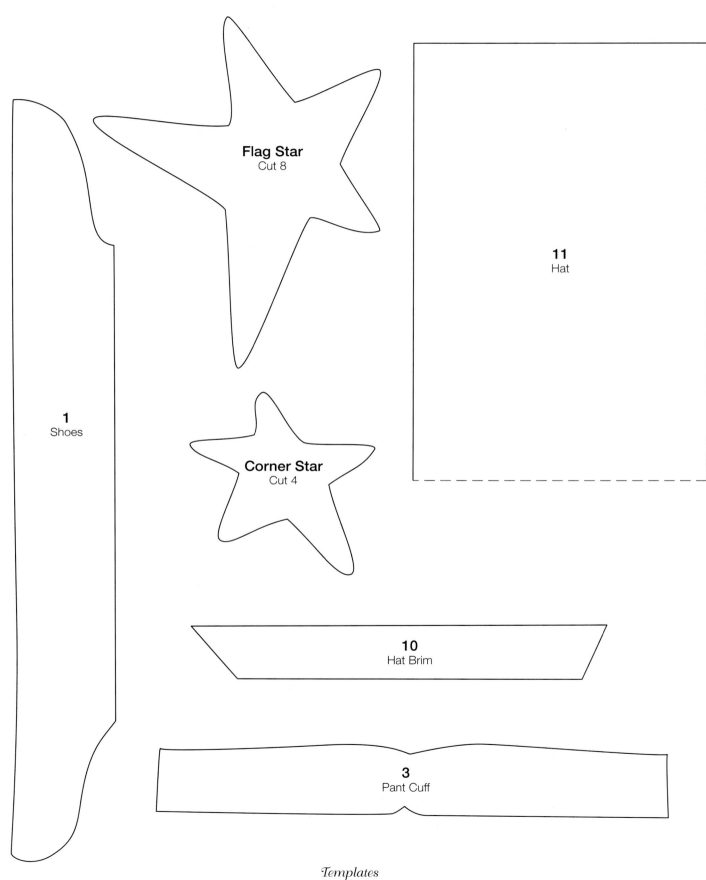

Flag Star
Cut 8

11
Hat

1
Shoes

Corner Star
Cut 4

10
Hat Brim

3
Pant Cuff

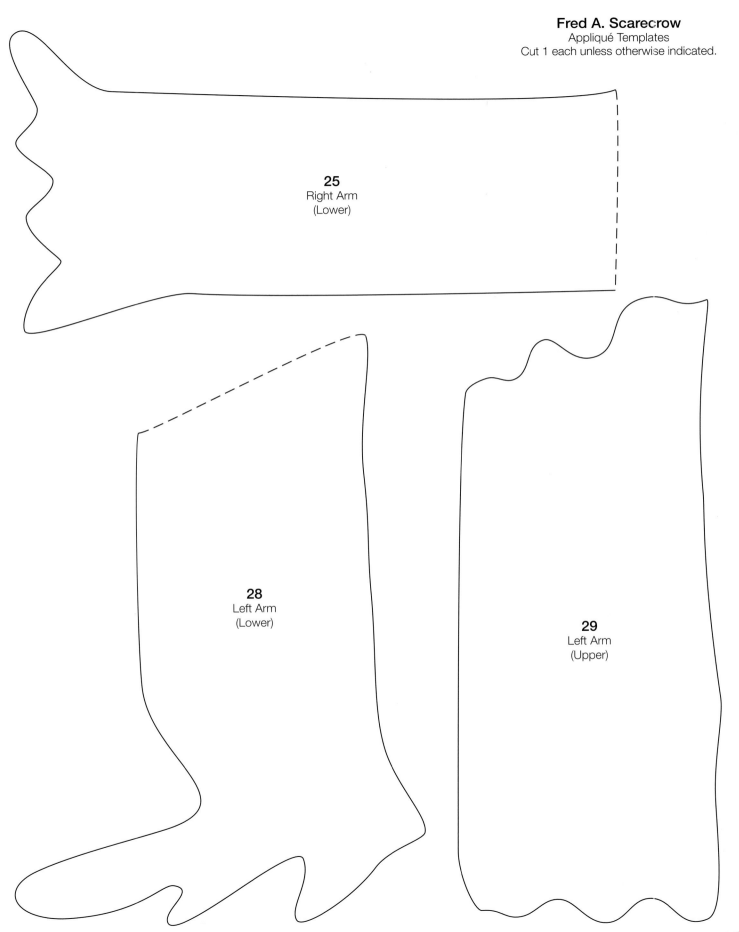

25
Right Arm
(Lower)

28
Left Arm
(Lower)

29
Left Arm
(Upper)

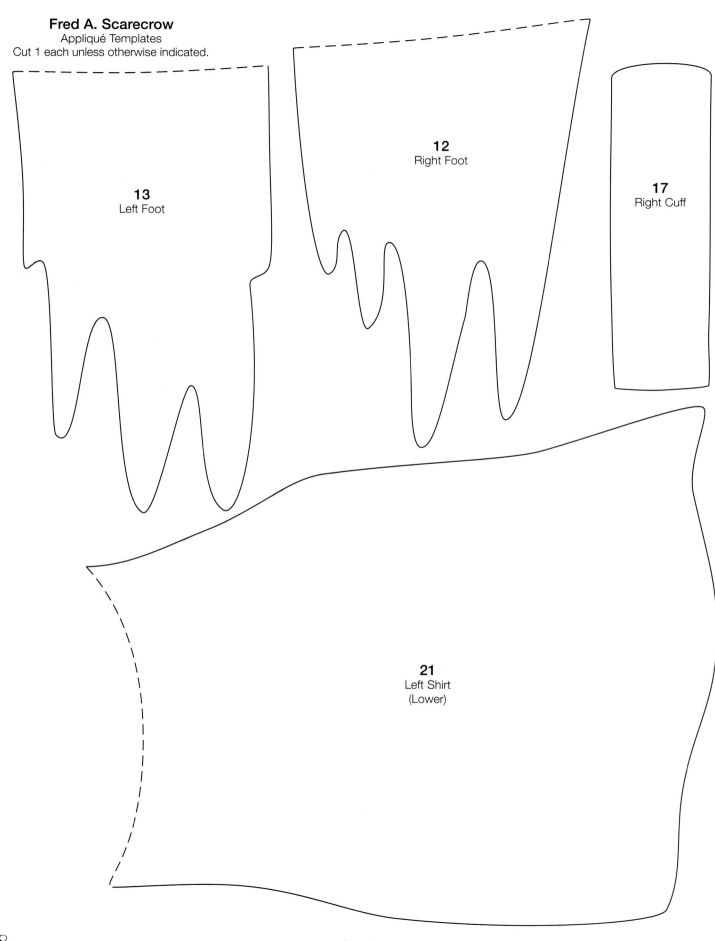

Fred A. Scarecrow
Appliqué Templates
Cut 1 each unless otherwise indicated.

13
Left Foot

12
Right Foot

17
Right Cuff

21
Left Shirt
(Lower)

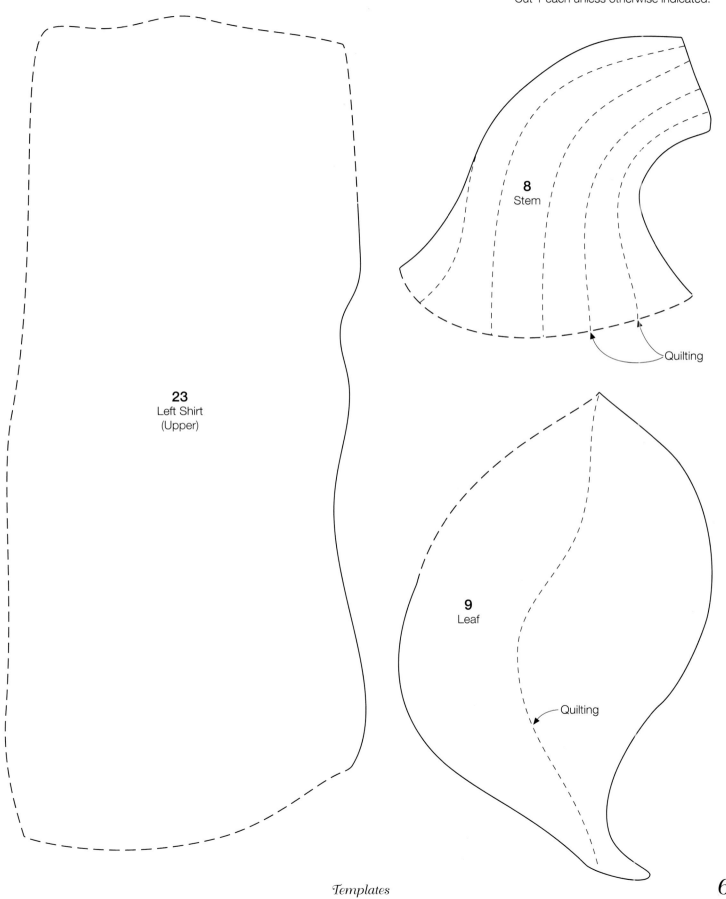

Fred A. Scarecrow
Appliqué Templates
Cut 1 each unless otherwise indicated.

8
Stem

Quilting

23
Left Shirt
(Upper)

9
Leaf

Quilting

Fred A. Scarecrow
Appliqué Templates
Cut 1 each unless otherwise indicated.

27
Left Hand

2
Pumpkin

Quilting

5
Stem

Quilting

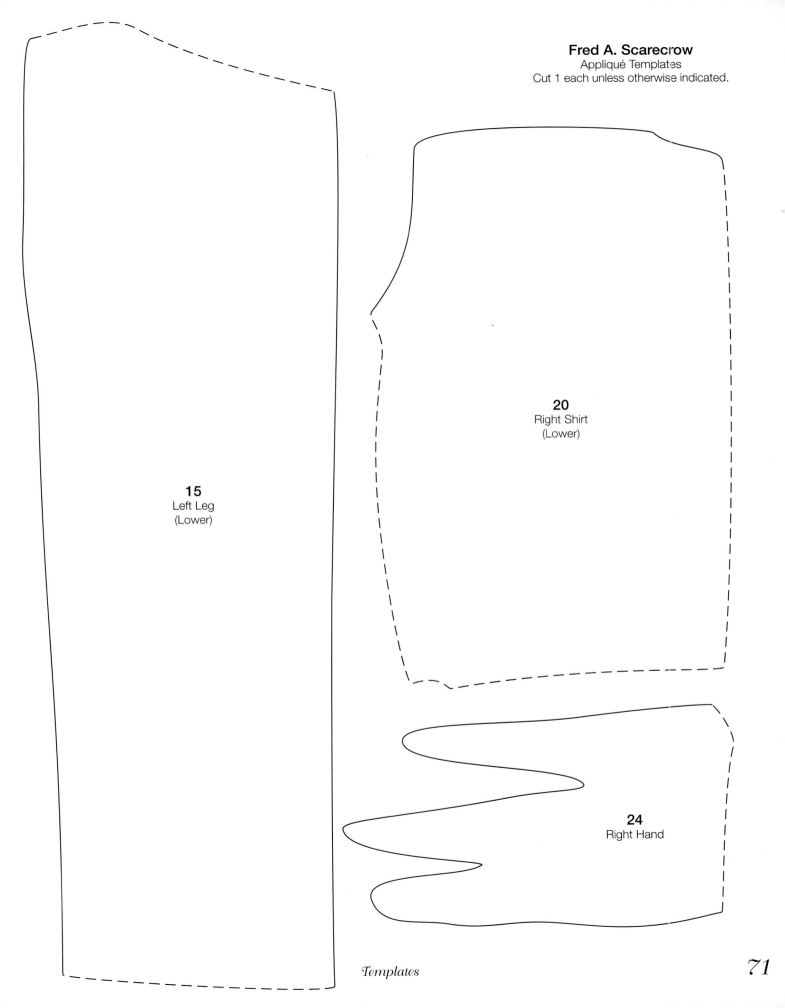

15
Left Leg
(Lower)

20
Right Shirt
(Lower)

24
Right Hand

Fred A. Scarecrow
Appliqué Templates
Cut 1 each unless otherwise indicated.

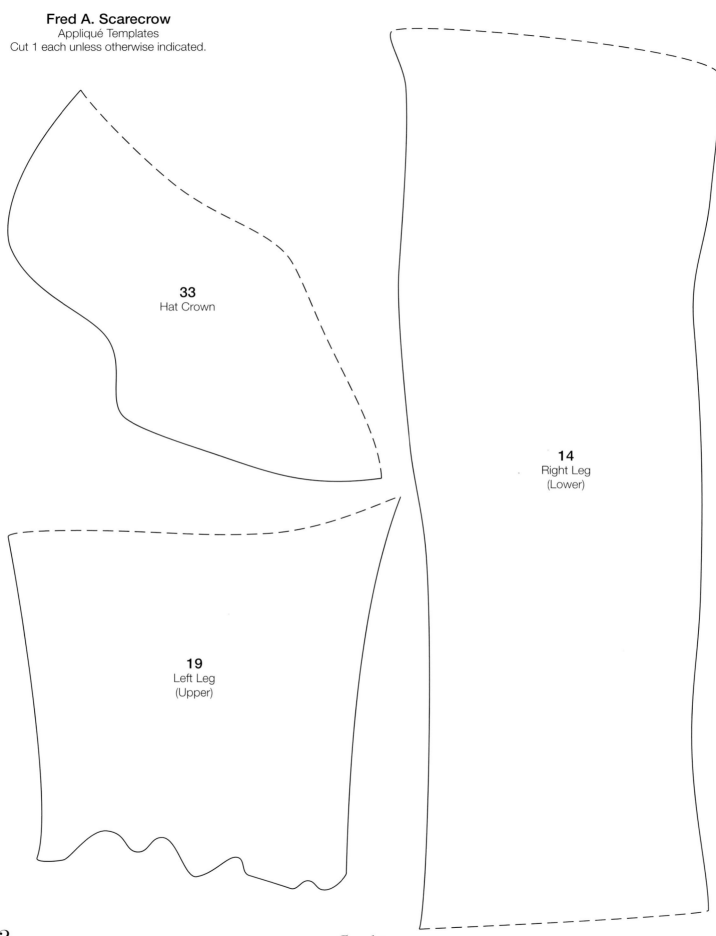

33
Hat Crown

14
Right Leg
(Lower)

19
Left Leg
(Upper)

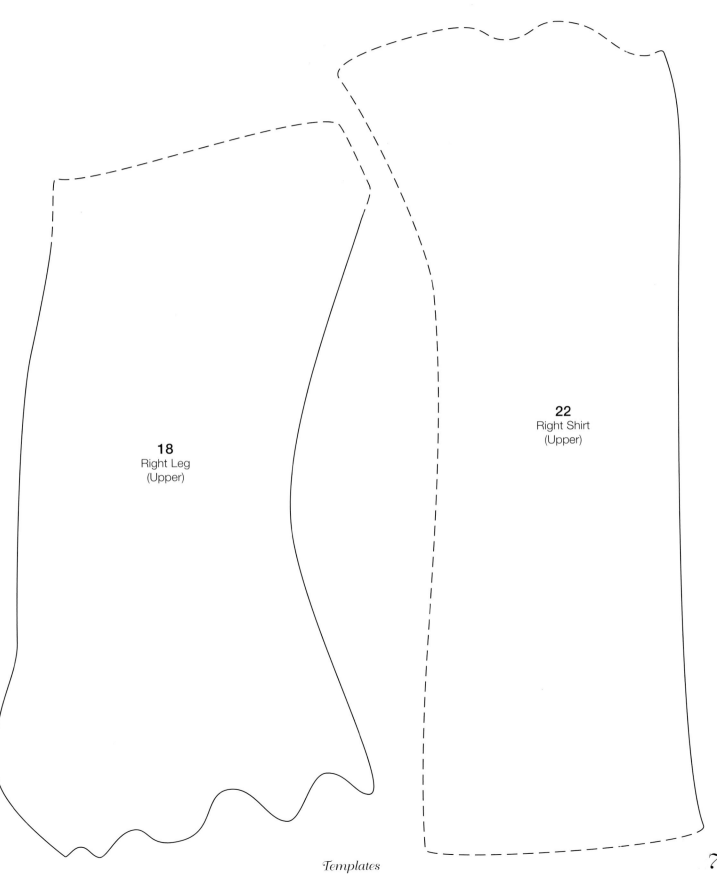

22
Right Shirt
(Upper)

18
Right Leg
(Upper)

Fred A. Scarecrow

Appliqué Templates
Cut 1 each unless otherwise indicated.

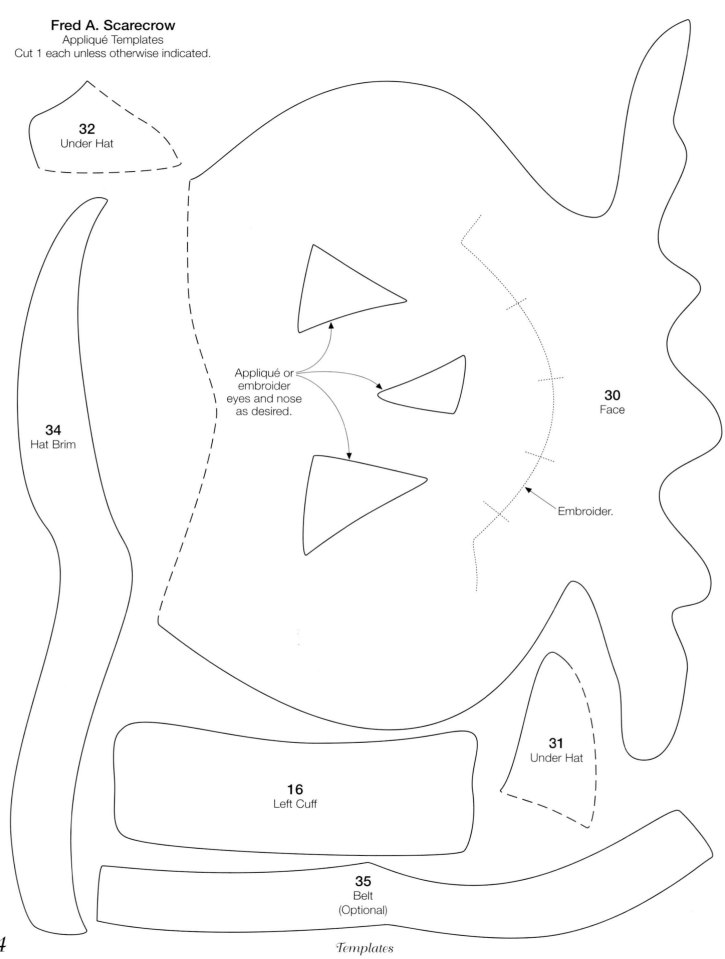

32
Under Hat

34
Hat Brim

Appliqué or
embroider
eyes and nose
as desired.

30
Face

Embroider.

31
Under Hat

16
Left Cuff

35
Belt
(Optional)

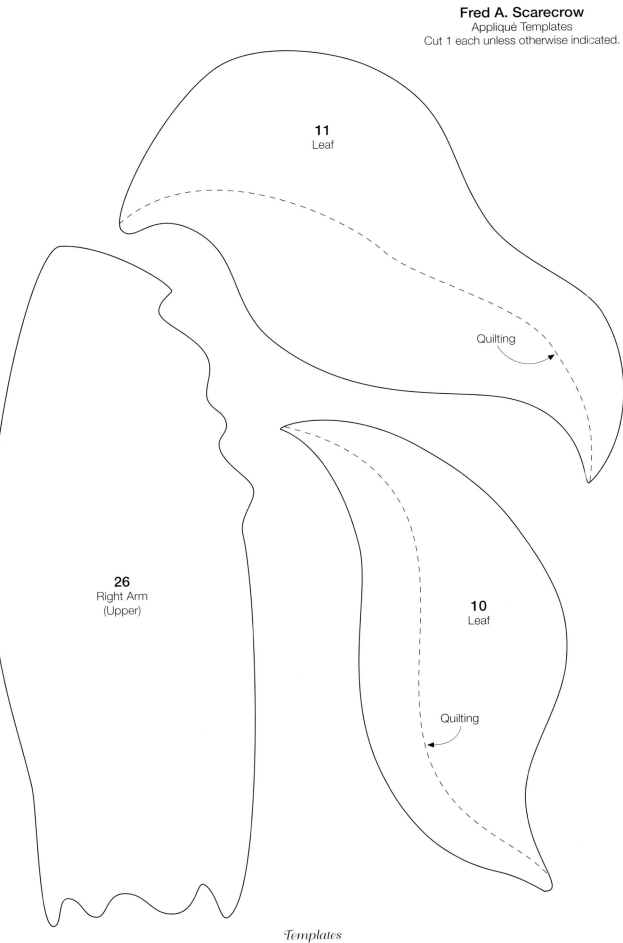

11
Leaf

Quilting

26
Right Arm
(Upper)

10
Leaf

Quilting

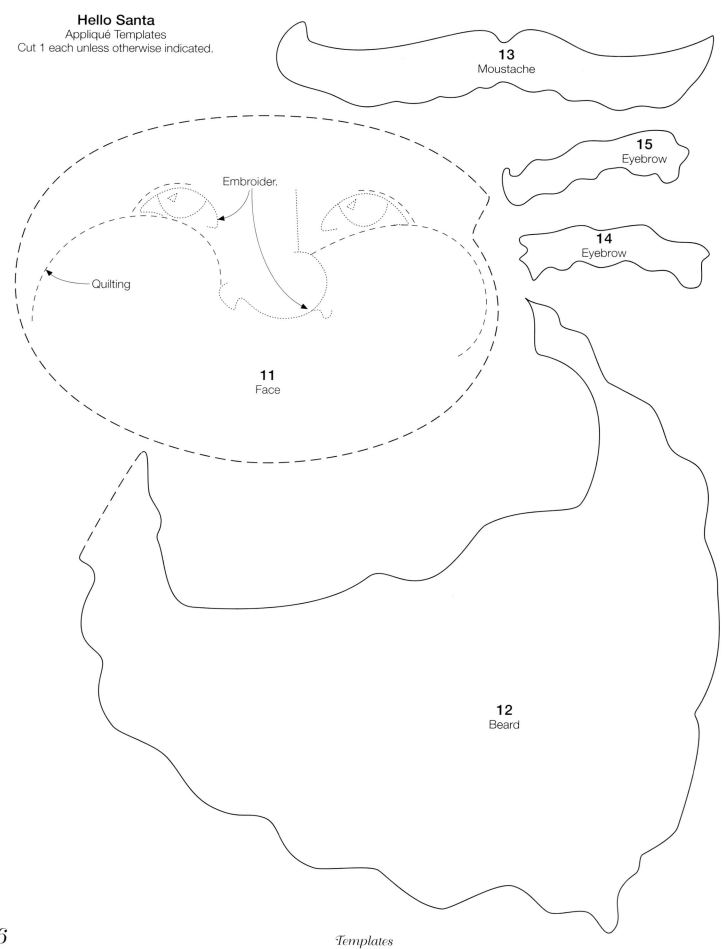

Hello Santa
Appliqué Templates
Cut 1 each unless otherwise indicated.

13
Moustache

15
Eyebrow

14
Eyebrow

Embroider.

Quilting

11
Face

12
Beard

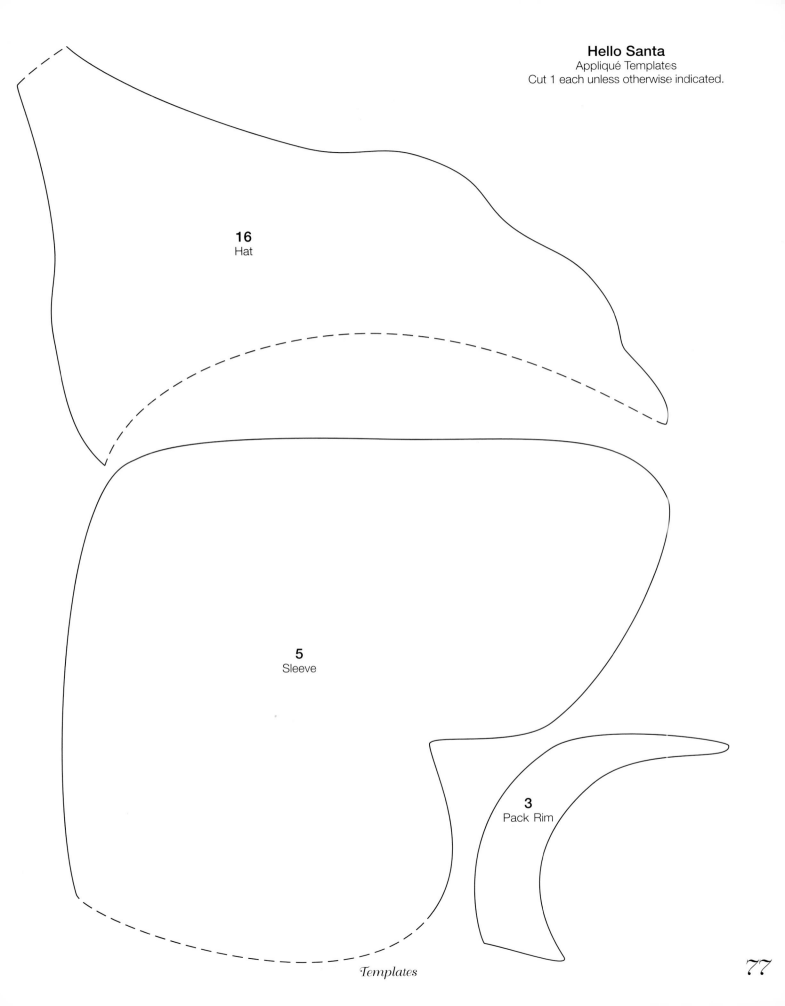

16
Hat

5
Sleeve

3
Pack Rim

Templates

About the Author

Lora Rocke grew up on the plains of Nebraska and acquired a love of art and needlework from her maternal grandmother. "Grammy" taught her a little bit of everything, but mostly she showed her how to improvise with color, design, and materials. Through the years, Lora has experimented with several art forms, from oil painting and batik to weaving and quilting. Wherever she roamed artistically, she always came back to fabrics and fibers. In 1972, Lora completed her first quilt from pieces begun by her great-grandmother.

Since then, Lora has taken classes, read books, and played. She has completed more than one hundred fifty projects, most of them machine pieced and quilted. "Quilting is very dynamic," Lora says. "I enjoy being able to produce a traditional art form quickly. Creating something both practical and beautiful is the best of both worlds."

Lora lives with her husband and daughter in Lincoln, Nebraska, where she creates, teaches, lectures, writes, and quilts. She is an active member of the Lincoln Quilters Guild, the Nebraska State Quilters Guild, and she joins friends in the Basket Cases and Celestial Quilters groups.

Notes

Publications and Products

Many titles are available at your local quilt shop.
For more information, write for a free color catalog
to That Patchwork Place, Inc., PO Box 118, Bothell,
WA 98041-0118 USA.

☎ U.S. and Canada, call 1-800-426-3126 for the
name and location of the quilt shop nearest you.
Int'l: 1-425-483-3313   Fax: 1-425-486-7596
E-mail: info@patchwork.com
Web: www.patchwork.com   7.97